T0079805

The Humboldt-Forum

PLANNING • PROCESSES • PERSPECTIVES

in the Berliner Schloss

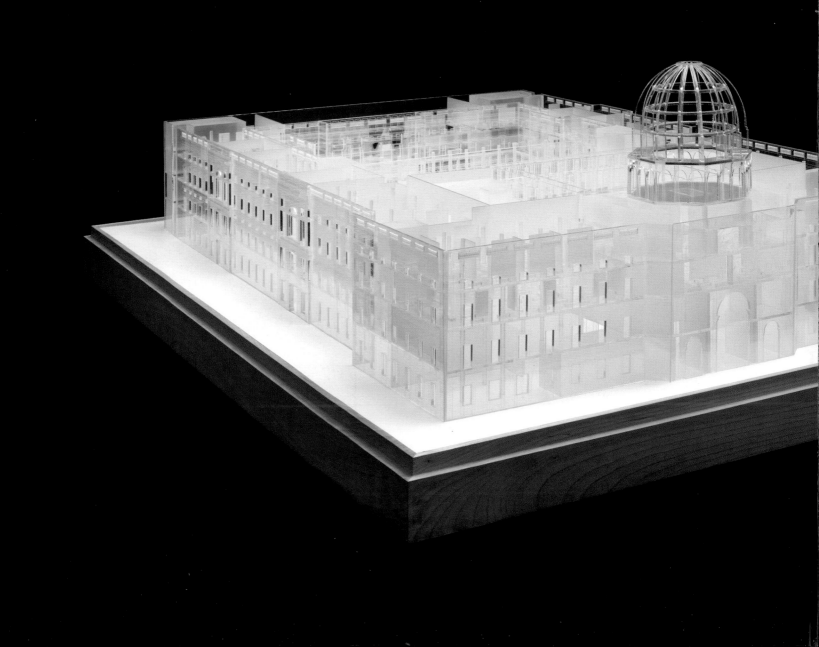

published by the
Stiftung Preußischer Kulturbesitz

HIRMER  Stiftung
Preußischer Kulturbesitz

Contents

Words of Welcome

**Bernd Neumann
Minister of State for
Culture and the Media**

The reconstruction of the Berliner Schloss will give our capital its historical centre once more. The project was preceded by a process of opinion making and discussion over a period of many years, which finally led in 2002 to a resolution in the Bundestag in favour of the palace with a broad majority of votes across all parties. Following the demolition of the residence of the Hohenzollern dynasty by the SED ruling powers and the Palast der Republik erected on the rubble, now for the first time in the many centuries of Berlin's history a democratically legitimated building will be created in the historic city centre. The name Humboldt-Forum refers to the best traditions of the Enlightenment. It stands for the links between aesthetics and science and at the same time for a liberal-minded rapprochement between cultures and the ideal of a peaceful dialogue between peoples.

Not far from the UNESCO World Heritage Site of the Museumsinsel, which represents the cultural heritage of Europe, a unique cultural and educational landscape, a true window on the cultures of the world will arise over the next few years. The project is being executed in cooperation with the non-European collections of the Staatliche Museen zu Berlin of the Stiftung Preußischer Kulturbesitz, together with the Zentral- und Landesbibliothek Berlin and the Humboldt-Universität zu Berlin. Through the combination of the museum and the scientific and library areas together with the event spaces on the ground floor, the exhibitions and events in the new building will complement and enrich each other. The Humboldt-Forum in the Berliner Schloss will be an ultra-modern centre for art, culture and science, a place of the present which does not deny the past and which embraces its treasures from a wide variety of perspectives and in a multiplicity of ways.

The laying of the foundation stone for the Humboldt Forum is cause for great rejoicing. A project which had been discussed almost into oblivion, in countless debates, is finally being realised, and a building housing a forward-looking centre of art, culture, science and education will definitely take shape in the historical centre of Berlin.

Berlin and Germany need the Humboldt-Forum. We need the idea of a dialogue of scholars and world cultures, a place which invites a broad public to examine the opportunities and risks of globalisation. Realising this project is important, because a commitment to cultural openness and the equality of the world's cultures corresponds to Germany's and Berlin's own cultural self-image.

The institutions involved can draw on a wealth of resources in realising this grand project. The collections of the Staatliche Museen zu Berlin are a unique treasure chest, as is the contribution of the Humboldt-Universität zu Berlin. And the Zentral- und Landesbibliothek Berlin will be adding another dimension to the Humboldt-Forum with its own media and knowledge.

Open-mindedness is a top priority at the Humboldt-Forum, and not only with regard to its exhibitions and programmes. The complex will be open to all – to children and young people, to the city's visitors, to Berliners of all backgrounds. A true place of world cultures will emerge here, in the heart of Berlin, in conjunction with the World Heritage site Museumsinsel. We hope it will provide orientation in our globalised world.

The contentious discussions in the past about the Humboldt-Forum were vital to the requisite sharpening of its profile. Let us hope that this institution remains the subject of public discussion, since that would attest to true interest, and indeed to true passion. And the Humboldt-Forum can never have enough of that.

Klaus Wowereit
Governing Mayor of Berlin

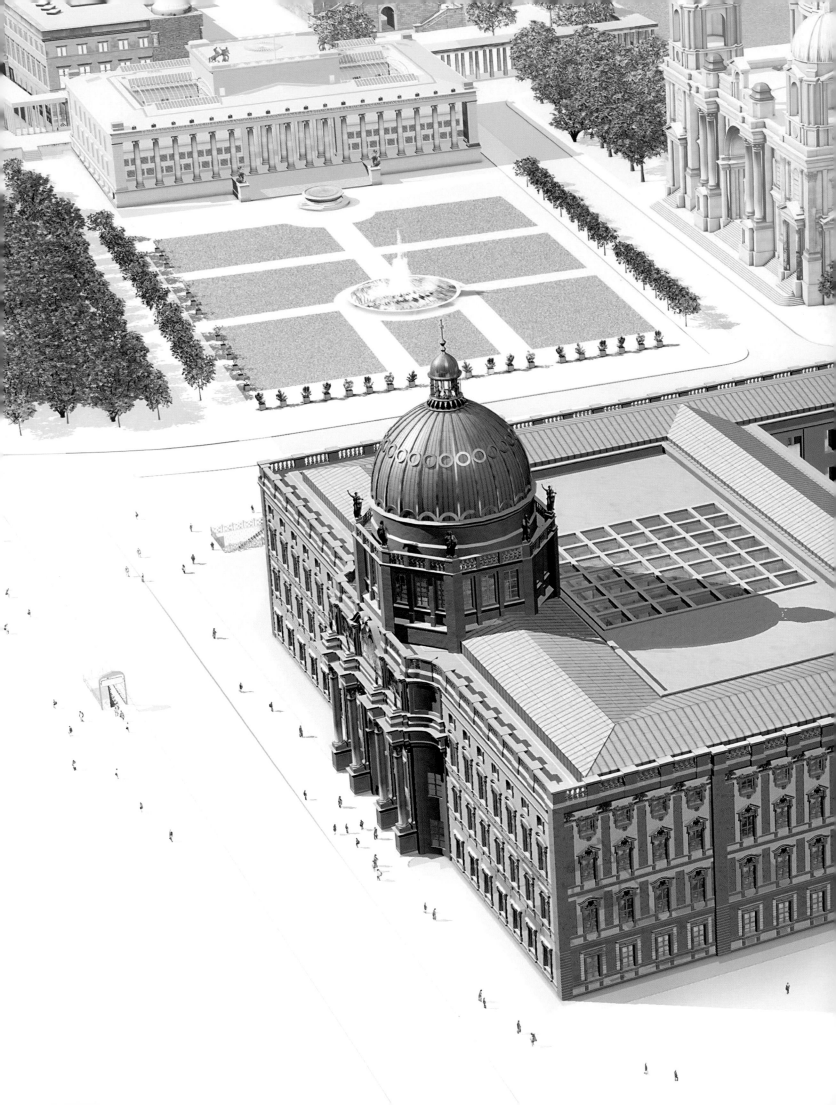

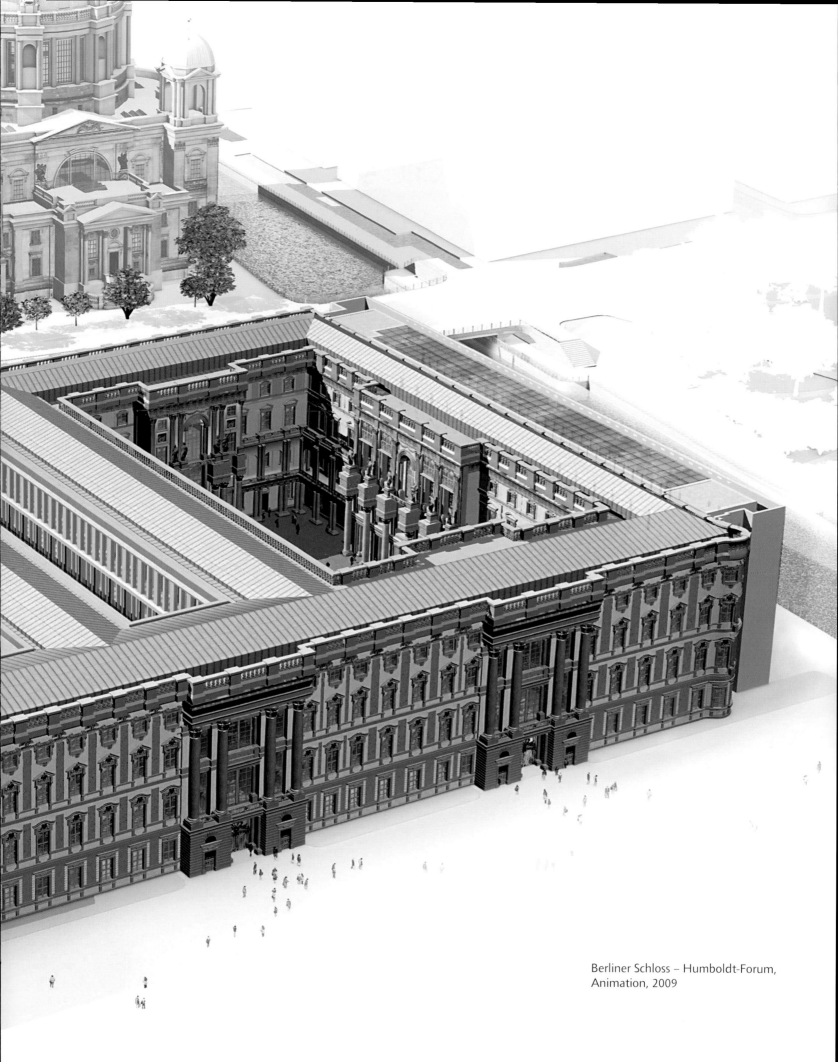

Berliner Schloss – Humboldt-Forum,
Animation, 2009

The Humboldt-Forum in the Berliner Schloss: Expectations and Opportunities

Hermann Parzinger

Rethinking the centre of Berlin from a cultural point of view

The fortunate reunification of Berlin following several decades of division has brought with it the great opportunity to re-design the historical centre of the capital city of Germany while drawing on Prussia's cultural accomplishments, and to rethink this centre from a cultural point of view, as was previously done in the nineteenth century. The outstanding cultural and artistic treasures of occidental tradition were gathered here, and from here scientific curiosity was directed at what was foreign and 'other' in the world. The aim is the development of this urban centre into one of the city's intellectual centres so that Berlin can become a true metropolis of the highest order.

The Museumsinsel (Museum Island) and its prominent collections of the art and culture of Europe and the Middle East were the great vision of the nineteenth century. On the other side of the Lustgarten a unique space for the art and culture of Asia, Africa, America, Australia and Oceania will be created with the Humboldt-Forum in the Berliner Schloss (Berlin Palace), which is being reconstructed. This ensemble will make Berlin one of the leading international cultural metropolises. It is possible because Berlin alone holds this wealth of collections from the entire world in one institution: the Staatliche Museen zu Berlin (National Museums in Berlin), which are part of the Stiftung Preußischer Kulturbesitz (Prussian Cultural Heritage Foundation). Only in Berlin, with the Museumsinsel and the Humboldt-Forum in close proximity to one another, is it possible to create a place dedicated to the cultures of the world that is as impressive as it is purposeful.

In this way we can express the intellectual willingness of our country to align the geographical heart of the historic centre of the German capital city with curiosity, dialogue and cosmopolitanism instead of with self involvement. And yet this place will also contribute to a sense of reassurance about ourselves in an increasingly globalised world. Cultural exchange on an equal footing must be the benchmark because Europe is by no means the world's interpretive centre any more. With the Humboldt-Forum Germany faces up to the task of reacting appropriately to the demands of a globalised world.

Transparent model of the Humboldt-Forum for exhibition design, Ralph Appelbaum Associates/malsyteufel, 2013

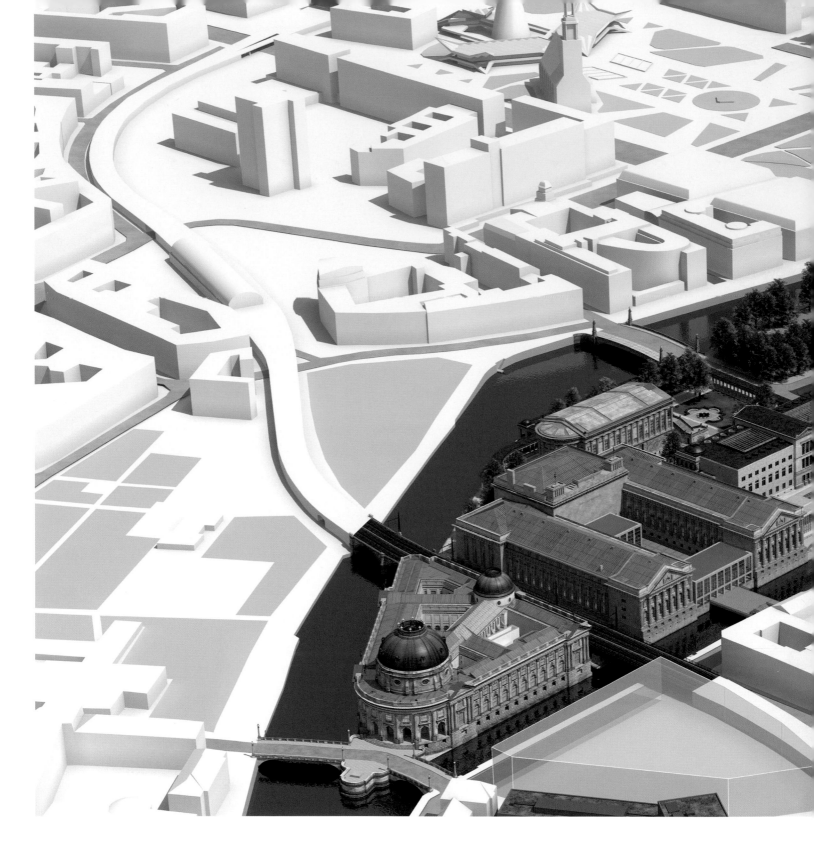

Museumsinsel in Berlin, with
a view of the future Berliner Schloss –
Humboldt-Forum, animation, 2012

"Everything is interaction," Alexander von Humboldt remarked long ago. On fertile soil such as this, knowledge about the world can grow. Knowledge and education are the keys to respect and tolerance towards other cultures, without which the peaceful coexistence of people would not be possible. This is also the extraordinarily humane message that underpins the *grand projet* of the Humboldt-Forum. In this way we draw on our tradition as a scientific and cultural nation, with recourse to the best of Prussia, and develop this into a new vision for the future.

One can see that cultural projects promote the reputation of metropolises worldwide, that they even have a profound influence on a nation's understanding of itself and help to form a sense of identity. Whether in Paris, London, Saint Petersburg, New York or Beijing, the strategy often consists of a powerfully symbolic combination of cultural heritage and forward-looking concepts.

There are many examples of world cities developing an almost magical attraction precisely when they are all about culture, and they blossom when their centres live and breathe culture. Nothing has a profounder effect on the image of a country in the world's eyes than that of its cultural centres.

The idea of the Humboldt-Forum is linked to the history of the Berliner Schloss

The concept of the Humboldt-Forum as a pioneering combination of museums, a library and a university has developed from the history of the place and for this reason has a special legitimacy: the museums, library and university collections grew from the residence of the Electors of Brandenburg and Kings of Prussia, and now return to their place of origin. The Hohenzollern palace was neither a citizens' forum nor a public library nor a much-visited museum. And yet art and science played a central role here from the beginning. The palace with its Brandenburg-Prussian Kunstkammer (cabinet of art and curiosities) was the site of an awakening of academic interest in nature and art. The ethnological collections that aimed to showcase the dynasty's cosmopolitanism and continent-spanning relationships were created in the palace. The idea of developing the Museumsinsel into a "sanctuary for art and science", to which end the royal museums, the newly founded university of Berlin and the Preußische Akademie der Wissenschaften (Prussian Academy of Sciences) would cooperate, was born in the palace.

Berliner Schloss, view across the Kupfergraben towards the west façade with the Eosanderportal, ca. 1910

The concept of the contents of the Humboldt-Forum therefore draws on the functions of the old palace, developing it in a modern manner. Its constituent elements are historically rooted in the palace, and this new palace in the form of the Humboldt-Forum stands for cosmopolitanism, equality, tolerance and democracy. A building that originally served the representation of power and politics is rededicated as a place of culture. German politics ordained this fundamental shift in its meaning after the reunification of Germany through decisions made by the German Bundestag in 2002 and 2003.

The forum shared by the museums, library and university is named for the brothers Wilhelm and Alexander von Humboldt, and both are considered leading figures for this new intellectual centre. Wilhelm stands for the importance of the classical history of ideas and intellectual history of Europe and for the understanding of non-European cultures; for the importance of language in understanding art and culture; for the connection of the museum, university and library; and for a far-reaching offensive in education policy. Alexander symbolises curiosity about the world; an open-minded description of foreign cultures; an interdisciplinary exploration of the continents; and the concept of an inseparable unity of nature and culture. Wilhelm, like Alexander, shaped a cosmopolitan view of the world that was based on a belief in the equality of all cultures. What was no more than an intellectual model upheld by a small number of people 200 years ago can today

Franco Stella, Berliner Schloss – Humboldt-Forum, view from Unter den Linden, rendering, 2013

Martin Paul Otto, Wilhelm von Humboldt, 1883, marble statue in front of the Humboldt-Universität, Unter den Linden

be implemented in a concrete manner in the centre of Berlin, and is entirely in keeping with Wilhelm von Humboldt's declaration that "the self wants to be in touch with as much world as possible."

The challenge of the Humboldt-Forum

The Humboldt-Forum in the Berliner Schloss features the unique opportunity to develop this burgeoning space of great historical significance, urban-planning accentuation and international charisma in Germany's capital city in a manner that is urbane, public and of high quality. It also features the possibility to give it a fascinating meaning: the cultures of the world effectively become participants in the most exclusive place in Germany. Thus Berlin and the entire country can rise to a challenge of international significance in a highly effective manner.

The Humboldt-Forum will communicate knowledge about the world, facilitate intercultural encounters and thus make people curious about what is foreign and different. In particular during a time when the cultures of the world collide with an unparalleled diversity, speed, intensity and complexity, the development of new forms of interaction with one another has become a central issue of our future coexistence. Understanding cultural multiplicity and a readiness for dialogue are essential prerequisites for a peaceful future. The Humboldt-Forum is essential because Germany needs a space for the exchange of views, aims and experiences from different kinds of cultures and societies, not least because of its growing economic and political significance. The centre of the capital city of Germany provides such a space, which does not yet exist in this way anywhere else. The Humboldt-Forum is therefore not only of importance for Berlin and for Germany, but can become important for the entire world.

The transformation of the demolished Hohenzollern palace into a place of world art and world culture and its dialogue with the sciences and the arts has a compelling inner logic: as though in a belated metamorphosis, the Prussian cultural state is being made visible here and makes its educational establishments fruitful for the future of a reunified Germany. Prussia's exceptional achievement, the wealth of collections of world art and culture gathered together in an encyclopaedic manner according to its educational ideals, will constitute the core of the Humboldt-Forum. Against the background of the cultural legacies, achievements and accomplishments from different times and different continents gathered together here, we will lend a voice to other cultures and in this way attempt a novel and contemporary interaction with the world.

The protagonists

Three institutions will shape the Humboldt-Forum: the Stiftung Preußischer Kulturbesitz, the Zentral- und Landesbibliothek Berlin (Central and Regional Library Berlin), and the Humboldt-Universität zu Berlin (Humboldt University of Berlin). The largest space will be occupied by the Stiftung Preußischer Kulturbesitz with the non-European collections of its Staatliche Museen zu Berlin, currently still located in Berlin-Dahlem: the Ethnologisches Museum (Ethnological Museum) and the Museum für Asiatische Kunst (Asian Art Museum). These collections contain considerably more than 500,000 artefacts and works of art from all continents, supplemented by unique sound and film documents. Together they form one of the richest collections of non-European art and culture worldwide. The Zentral- und Landesbibliothek Berlin features an extensive service area and will be dedicated to the subject of the "World of Languages". The third partner, the Humboldt-Universität zu Berlin, has planned a Humboldt-Labor (Humboldt Laboratory) with temporary exhibitions and events on particular subjects. The Humboldt-Forum will be a place where the world as a whole can be consulted while creating a space for in-depth specialisation. The principle of thinking about the future in global terms is already incorporated into the history of the palace.

The concept features the unique possibility to create novel links between the participating institutions, to develop forms of complementary cooperation, and to create points of access to the world that go beyond the narrow boundaries of the classic disciplines. The arts and sciences will enter into a dialogue and present a rich selection of cultural activities to the public. The occidental view of the world will be complemented by additional perceptions and therefore provoke a shift in perspective. In this special, innovative combination of art and culture, science and education, the Humboldt-Forum will give the metropolis of Berlin a new intellectual centre and simultaneously keep the entire world in its view, in keeping with the spirit of the von Humboldt brothers.

Reinhold Begas, Alexander von Humboldt, 1883, marble statue in front of the Humboldt-Universität, Unter den Linden

The history of the collections

The non-European collections of Berlin are among the biggest and most important of their kind worldwide. In their specific composition they provide a multifaceted basis for an engagement with the art and cultural history of Africa, America, Asia, Australia and Oceania, always including the ambivalent relationships with the Europeans. Nowadays the descendants of those peoples whose legacies were collected in previous centuries are increasingly interested in these holdings. They regard them as important evidence of their history, and in many cases they are the only documents of their kind to have survived colonisation, missionary work and modernisation unscathed. The Berlin collections not only document the past, but also provide important anchor points in the search for cultural identity.

The foundation for a systematic collection of non-European art and culture was laid by explorers: Georg Forster accompanied James Cook to the South Seas, Alexander von Humboldt examined the natural and cultural history of Latin America, and Hermann Schlagintweit travelled through Tibet and Mongolia. They and many others collected objects and brought them back to Berlin from their travels. Their reports were published in books and shown as films, and their stories were retold for children, so that an interest in the scientific quest for knowledge was awakened in the younger generation.

The foundation of the Königliches Museum für Völkerkunde (Royal Museum of Ethnology) by Adolf Bastian in the year 1873 was a milestone in the systematic examination and understanding of the cultures of the world. Bastian had made it his aim to document the already endangered cultures of foreign continents, to collect evidence as comprehensively as possible, and to preserve this for future generations. The establishment of German colonies in Africa and the South Seas increased the steady flow of objects from these parts of the world, and yet the balance and completeness of the Berlin collections

Humboldt-Forum in the Berliner
Schloss, animation, 2009

Stores in the Ethnologisches Museum, 2010

can be traced back to a skilfully planned network of collectors and purchasers, established by Bastian, that spread across the world. The scientific foundation of our present-day engagement with the cultures of the world was created at that time.

The Ostasiatische Kunstsammlung (Department of East Asian Art), whose establishment in 1906 was driven by Wilhelm von Bode, grew out of a different approach. Ahead of its time, it was among the first to aim to show the equal status of occidental and oriental art in the early twentieth century. Berlin set new standards in the world of museums with this novel approach. The backbone of the collection was created by an active acquisitions practice and thanks to bourgeois patronage. It was joined by the former Museum für Indische Kunst (Museum of Indian Art) from 1963, and together they have formed the Museum für Asiatische Kunst since 2006.

The non-European collections of the Staatliche Museen zu Berlin – Preußischer Kulturbesitz (Prussian Cultural Heritage), divided up between the Ethnologisches Museum and the Museum für Asiatische Kunst, have been housed in Dahlem, on the southwest periphery of Berlin, since World War II. This museum location once encompassed significant holdings of the Staatliche Museen (National Museums) in West Berlin, which constituted a delightful little universal museum of sorts there at the time. This provisional arrangement due to the separation of Germany lost a considerable degree of its charm as a result of the development of the Kulturforum Potsdamer Platz and the recovery of the Museumsinsel following the reunification of Germany. Important collections such as the Gemäldegalerie (Old Master Paintings), the Kupferstichkabinett (Museum of Prints and Drawings), the Skulpturensammlung (Sculpture Collection) and the Museum für Islamische Kunst (Museum of Islamic Art) were moved from Dahlem to new buildings on Potsdamer Strasse or to their previous locations in the centre of Berlin. What remained in Dahlem was the neglected torso of non-European art and culture that had been robbed of the opportunity for any juxtaposition with the arts and cultures of Europe and the Middle East. The aim is to recreate this unity, but in an entirely new dimension.

Overcoming hierarchies and creating connections

Moving the non-European collections from Dahlem to the centre of Berlin and displaying them in proximity to the Museumsinsel will reintegrate them into an ensemble in which they will be freed of the stigma of the exotic. This, too, is part of the equality of presentation and perception of world cultures. It is abundantly clear that those interested in culture and visitors to museums have long since begun to think in global dimensions. The Musée du Quai Branly in Paris was opened in 2006 as an exceptional space of non-European art and culture in France, and continuously sets new records with its visitor numbers; the Louvre has a gallery of masterpieces of non-European art; and the British Museum in London has integrated important departments of the arts and cultures of Africa, Asia and America. Overcoming the hierarchies that have long been inappropriate between the arts and cultures of the world is one of the great challenges of our time. These universal museums in particular are the ones that must confront this challenge, and they must do so in close dialogue with the international community and an increasingly multi-ethnic society.

In 1995 the former French president Jacques Chirac made the astute observation that the Louvre could not remain a truly great museum in the future if it continued to ignore the art of 70 percent of the world's population. The exceptional quality of the non-European collections of the Staatliche Museen zu Berlin – Preußischer Kulturbesitz supports this statement in an important way. They encompass masterpieces of world art from all continents. Commemorative heads made from the European import brass and relief plaques from the West African country of Benin continue to fascinate viewers with their exceptional artistic quality. The magnificent feather adornments made of colourful parrot feathers from the Amazon were already admired by visitors to the Kunstkammer in the Berliner Schloss. The stone figures of the gods of the Aztecs and relief steles of the Maya weighing several tonnes bring to life the imaginative worlds of the pre-Columbian cultures of Mesoamerica. The suggestive expressive power of wood figures from islands in the vicinity of Papua New Guinea had a lasting effect on the German Expressionists. The ever-changing presentation of Chinese and Japanese painting reflects the change of seasonal, religious and social events, which will allow the visitor to experience various aspects of the visual culture of East Asia. Central Asian Gandharan sculptures carry viewers off into a fascinating world in which Greco-Roman-influenced art lives on in an environment shaped

Polychrome cylinder vase with war scene, Mexico, Mayan culture, 600–900

by Buddhism along the route of the Silk Road. The world of Islam becomes comprehensible as a phenomenon spanning the continents, and establishes a connection to the Museumsinsel. And Europe, too, will always also be present in the Humboldt-Forum in the form of well-founded interventions.

New windows on the arts and cultures of the world

Selected exhibits and subjects will guide the visitors in the exhibition areas of the Humboldt-Forum on their journeys through the world, opening up new ways of understanding cultural connections in the process. The presentation of art and material culture starts with temporary exhibitions on the ground floor and continues in two rooms for large objects on the first floor before our collections of the cultures and arts of the world unfold their full glory on the second and third floors. The presence of every continent will unfold in its full visual, acoustic and sensual variety. Cultural continuities spanning space and time are revealed, as are the shaping forces of the environment and the paths humans have taken to overcome the boundaries set for them by nature. Documentation of everyday life, of religious culture and artistic creation, of the spirit of technical innovation, ecological and economical conditions and the always-present trans-continental connections combine to form a unique panorama of civilisations.

Objects provide the unique opportunity to understand history in a special way because they speak of global developments during the time of their creation: they bear witness to their times. Quite ordinary things can play a significant role in that they were created by humans like us. This insight provides the viewer with new forms of access to a deeper understanding of global interactions. The aim is to allow the exhibits to unfold their aesthetic effects while positioning them within their cultural contexts and letting them tell their own stories. Both those interested in art and searching for aesthetic experiences and those interested in religion and cultural history will recognise that the Humboldt-Forum is a space intended for them.

The aim is not to create a classic permanent exhibition but an open, permeable, changeable structure that draws on the multiplicity, changes, possibilities and risks of our time and reflects current aspects of the collections in an ambitious manner. One objective is to explain the fundamental mechanisms of human action from a historical perspective. Another is to supplement this view with perspectives rooted in the present through contemporary interpretations of the old, through the most modern forms of communication and through contemporary-art interventions; by confronting these objects of the past with current questions to establish connections with the people of today. Special exhibitions that are dedicated to central issues of our time and shine a new light on such phenomena as globalisation, migration, climate change and mega-cities will play an important role in this context. Many of these problems that move the world of today are in no way new, and are among the prominent side effects of human development: they are the great issues of humankind.

In the presentation of objects of cultural significance it is important to create a variety of points of access. It is no longer sufficient to accentuate the European view of the world. The interpretive prerogative of European academics in museums has long been

Commemorative head of a queen mother, Nigeria, Kingdom of Benin, early 16th century

called into question by post-colonial criticism. Now is the time to draw the appropriate conclusions.

Tendencies to exoticise or re-exoticise all that is foreign are diametrically opposed to the Humboldt-Forum's commitment to an egalitarian approach to the arts and cultures of the world. A wide variety of participants, and particularly indigenous groups and artists from the various countries of origin are therefore to be included in the constant re-interpretation of objects and their narrative presentation. In a change of perspective of sorts, their knowledge can enrich our approach to the collections because they add new points of view and different types of knowledge. In this way, multiple perspectives and a variety of voices will become part of the Humboldt-Forum's fundamental position with regard to its contents. Only thus can we objectify our own view of the world. There is no conflict in this critical self-reflection of the museum's position, but it provides instead tremendous potential for the further development of our traditional cultural institutions.

Zhang Lu, Playing the Zither for One's Friend, Ming dynasty, 1st half of the 16th century

A place for orientation and world expertise

The Werkstätten des Wissens (Workshops of Knowledge), the Humboldt-Forum's area for science and research, are concentrated on the top floor. It is here that the museums, library and university will work together and draw upon each other's work in their specific contributions to the Humboldt-Forum. In conjunction with national and international partners the Humboldt-Forum will develop into a centre for research and

Skanda/Kartikeya, India, Orissa,
13th century

communication of world art and culture that reaches beyond the confines of individual subjects and institutions. The natural and intellectual bases of worldwide cultural variety will be explored here, and communicated to the public in the most modern way possible, using electronic and print media, to form an interactive meeting with global knowledge about the world.

The collections and the research libraries and archives of the Ethnologisches Museum and of the Museum für Asiatische Kunst, and the sourcing of academic information by the Zentral- und Landesbibliothek Berlin, will provide the starting point for this. The development of scientific findings will be vividly displayed to visitors at the Humboldt-Labor of the Humboldt-Universität zu Berlin. The intersection of the three partners – museums, library and university – are particularly numerous here, and allow the three institutions to become interconnected. The non-European collections of the Staatliche Museen zu Berlin – Preußischer Kulturbesitz and the relevant academic collections of the Humboldt-Universität, for example, will complement one another. The Lautarchiv (Sound Archive) of the Humboldt-Universität complements the Phonogramm-Archiv (Phonogram Archive) of the Ethnologisches Museum, a unique collection of languages, music and voices from all the continents that was recorded more than 100 years ago on a total of 16,000 wax cylinders and that has been adopted by the UNESCO's Memory of the World list.

The specific contribution to the Humboldt-Forum of the Zentral- und Landesbibliothek Berlin forms an ideal addition: a language library that draws on the seminal works of Wilhelm von Humboldt and makes language become comprehensible as a many-faceted phenomenon and integral constituent part of cultural and social structures. The Humboldt-Forum will be a place of communication and integration; in this respect it is essential to sensitise ourselves to linguistic variety and to make media and resources for language acquisition available. This is why the Zentral- und Landesbibliothek will not only accompany and expand the exhibitions and events in the Humboldt-Forum from the point of view of content, but also establish networks that reach beyond: the language library of the Humboldt-Forum will be an attractive point of contact for linguistic research networks, as well as developing a social effect through advisory work in linguistic didactics.

Berlin is an exceptional location on an international level, with great expertise in the sphere of regional studies. For these fields of study the Humboldt-Forum will be a place in which they can come together and become visible in the form of subject-specific, interdisciplinary associations. Here they will be able to develop trans-regional dimensions and simultaneously generate knowledge to aid orientation and translation that will deepen our understanding of the interplay of the various regions of the world. International, transdisciplinary teams of researchers composed of ethnologists, sociologists, climatologists and representatives of other subjects will also develop new forms for the presentation of knowledge. The Humboldt-Forum will be a very lively place for the cooperation of scientists and artists in particular, including new formats of artistic research. Such knowledge should be available not only to specialists, however, but should also be projected out at those members of the public who have an interest in it because accessibility and the communication of the constantly growing body of knowledge about the world are among the most distinguished roles of the Humboldt-Forum.

Humboldt Lab Dahlem, Probe-
bühne 1 (Rehearsal Stage 1),
Project Springer "Purnakumbha",
March 2013

Eyak Mask, Alaska, Cooper River, before 1882

International groups of researchers made up of renowned scholars and excellent young academics will dedicate themselves to fundamental questions of humankind in the framework of research and funding programmes. The Humboldt-Forum will be a place of creation for scientists in residence and artists in residence, and will thus establish new possibilities for exchange and fruitful cooperation between the sciences and the arts. And all of this will take place in a manner much more visible to the public than is the case elsewhere. Visitors to the Humboldt-Forum will discover how knowledge about the world is developed.

At the Humboldt-Forum the museums, library and university will cooperate closely in the sphere of cultural education. All sections of our society, and particularly children and young people, are to be introduced to art and culture in a special way, and they are to be equipped to formulate independently new realisations through the transmission of information expertise. Through the cooperation of cultural, educational and research facilities and a complementary programme of events organised together with the Schülerakademie (Pupils' Academy), junior museums and centres of learning, the distinctive characteristics of the cultures of Africa, the Americas, Asia, Australia and Oceania can be communicated in the context of their interactions with Europe. This will be done with a variety of focal points and by making use of all media relating to text and pictorial culture, theatre, music and film. Knowledge will be made available in the Humboldt-Forum in a modern and comprehensive manner. Without knowledge there can be no understanding and no openness to communication.

On the multiplicity of forms of cultural expression

The ground floor of the Humboldt-Forum is dedicated to the present and the multiplicity of forms of cultural expression. The visitor is welcomed and prepares for a fascinating voyage of experience and discovery in the western entrance hall in what used to be the Eosanderhof courtyard. This roofed hall is the gravitational centre of the entire Humboldt-Forum. The tremendous height of the ceiling reflects the dimensions of the historic palace. The entrance hall is a meeting place for visitors from around the world, providing information about what is on offer and directing them to other parts of the building. Circumferential galleries on all three storeys are the stage for an ensemble that aims to remind visitors of the former Kunstkammer that was the seed from which the Humboldt-Forum has grown. Developments from the history of ideas and intellectual history are taken up and incorporated into an echo chamber that reaches to the present day. The Kunstkammer is thus transported into a modern macrocosm in a microcosm. It no longer attempts to astonish visitors with its exotic curiosities and rarities, but instead attempts to interest them in a dialogue among equals with the cultures of the world by presenting them with objects that bear witness to the exchange that has taken place throughout the centuries. This is simultaneously the fundamental difference between the Kunstkammer and the Humboldt-Forum.

The ground floor will be dedicated primarily to topical subjects of the present day. It will also house an exhibition on the history of the place that reminds of and reflects on significant historical and architectural stages in the development of the Schlossplatz, and a walk-in Archaeological Window through which one can descend into the depths of the history of the Berliner Schloss and experience part of the original structure of the historic building. Spaces for temporary exhibitions, multifunctional spaces, an auditorium and a repertory cinema are designed for events in the fields of art, theatre, film, music, literature and performance. Film has long since become a global medium that unfolds its creative power in a very special way. Classic and experimental theatre will make popular traditions in the performing arts from all over the world come alive and be comprehensible to a wide public. A stage for musical performances can bring worlds of sound from the continents to the heart of Berlin and in this way establish connections between traditional music programmes and contemporary forms. Special exhibitions will allow visitors to experience the newest of developments in contemporary art from Africa, America and Asia and, like seismographs, show up social developments. Subjects of present-day relevance from the fields of science, society, culture and politics will be debated by designated experts in the Humboldt-Forum as a forum dedicated to the word.

Rethinking the world from the point of view of culture

The Humboldt-Forum's added value lies in its multiplicity, liveliness and topicality, which provide it with the characteristics of a public and participatory space for dialogue with the world's cultures, in keeping with the idea of a "house of the people". The Humboldt-Forum will be unique in that these activities will radiate throughout the entire building and all of its areas. The challenge and opportunity lies not in the addition of its constituent parts, but in their successful integration. The offerings must also take into account a public of increasingly diverse social and cultural origins. This applies both to the selection of themes and subjects, and also to the planning of varied dramaturgies, intentional ruptures and tensional arcs and experimental spaces for various age and social groups in all parts of the Humboldt-Forum so that it can – in keeping with Humboldtian philosophy – "delight and instruct".

The success of the Humboldt-Forum will be measured by its visitors. The public's expectations vary according to their origins and motivations, and they will change over the course of the years, just as society and the world will change. The Humboldt-Forum must follow this developmental process, and it must always remain part of the process and try to have an influence on these changes. This will be its particular challenge. The Humboldt-Forum must become a place that offers people knowledge which they can use to orient themselves. To this end it will not only provoke and organise relevant discourses, but also take into account current requirements. Only then can uncertainty be transformed into expertise and curiosity about the world lead to new forms of engagement with other people and cultures.

In this way the Humboldt-Forum can develop into a supranational institution that is used by the entire world. This will allow Germany to make an important contribution to peaceful cohesion and reciprocal understanding amongst the peoples of a long-since globalised world. An exceptional place in which the entire world will be united culturally will thus come into being in the centre of Berlin in the form of the Museumsinsel and the Humboldt-Forum, whose contents together form a single entity. The very humane power of culture will unfold its effect from here: it will enable people to gain reassurance about themselves and it will communicate world expertise.

How it Began: From the Palast der Republik to the Berliner Schloss – Humboldt-Forum

Manfred Rettig

Palast der Republik, ca. 1986

The reconstruction of the Berliner Schloss (Berlin Palace) has a long history, essentially dating back to the reunification of Germany. Discussions about the future of the site began with a decision by the Volkskammer (People's Chamber) of the German Democratic Republic in September 1990 to close the Palast der Republik (Palace of the Republic) because of protests by employees about high levels of asbestos contamination, and confirmation by experts that it was acutely dangerous. Following the reunification of Germany the Umzugsstab Berlin (Berlin Relocation Task Force) under my leadership also developed proposals for removing the asbestos from the palace, to which there was no technical alternative. An attempt was made to find a feasible utilisation concept for the Palast der Republik following refurbishment. An Expression of Interest procedure was launched in the 1990s, but it remained inconclusive. Discussions were also held with figures from politics, culture, the economy and the media as part of the so-called Petersberger Gespräche (Petersburg Discussions) in Bonn to find possible uses for the shell of the palace building, but without result.

The search for possible public-sector occupants revealed the need for considerable maintenance work on the federal Dahlem-based museums of the Stiftung Preußischer Kulturbesitz (Prussian Cultural Heritage Foundation). On the recommendation of the Umzugsstab Berlin all construction measures in Dahlem were postponed pending a decision about the Palast der Republik, so that the financial savings could be invested in its after-use and the Dahlem property could later be sold. The Zentral- und Landesbibliothek Berlin (Central and Regional Library Berlin) was the second public institution that might occupy the space because of a little-known construction feature: the Palast der Republik and the Marstall were connected by a subterranean passage. The idea was to expand the existing facilities of the Zentral- und Landesbibliothek in Breite Strasse through the addition of the Marstall building, to construct a book-transportation system in the subterranean passage, and to house the prestigious and attractive part of the library in the facility that would

Franco Stella, architectural competition
2007, model for the Berliner Schloss

follow the Palast der Republik. The sale of the Amerika-Gedenkbibliothek (America Memorial
Library) at Hallesches Ufer, which was in need of repair, could contribute to the finances.

The palace simulation set up in front of the Palast der Republik by the Förderverein
Berliner Schloss e. V. (Association Berliner Schloss) in 1993/94 shifted the public discussion
from the future use of the Palast der Republik to the reconstruction of the Berliner Schloss,
and therefore to a political discussion about the approach to historical buildings in general
and those of the former German Democratic Republic in particular. A lengthy public debate followed.

In the late 1990s an international commission of experts was tasked with developing
of a concept for the palace-square area. The Umzugsstab Berlin provided the members
with the architectural and usage proposals received until that point. After several sessions
the commission recommended the reconstruction of the historic external façade of the
Berliner Schloss – with the exception of the east façade – and the reconstruction of the
three façades of the inner courtyard of the Schlüterhof. The idea of the Humboldt-Forum
was developed as a usage concept.

A forum for a dialogue between the cultures of the world is to be created in the
heart of the German capital. It will draw on the Kunstkammer (cabinet of art and curiosities) that existed in the Berliner Schloss from the sixteenth century, and will be based on
cooperation between the institutions of the Stiftung Preußischer Kulturbesitz, the Zentral-
und Landesbibliothek Berlin and the Humboldt-Universität zu Berlin (Humboldt University
of Berlin). The erstwhile seat of political power over several centuries will now become a
place that belongs to the people, and a symbol of the peaceful collaboration of cultures.

This persuasive, forward-looking concept achieved a broad, cross-party majority in the German Bundestag. The international architectural competition of 2007 was won a year later by the Italian architect Franco Stella.

Preparatory construction began in mid 2012 so that the tunnel construction for Line 5 of the Berlin Underground can go ahead under the Humboldt-Forum until mid 2014. The laying of the foundation stone in June 2013 will mark the beginning of the construction of the Humboldt-Forum itself, and its completion is scheduled for early 2018. The opening is to take place in 2019. Founded in 2009, the Stiftung Berliner Schloss – Humboldtforum (Berliner Palace – Humboldtforum Foundation) is the awarding authority and owner of this, the most significant cultural project of the Federal Republic of Germany since the beginning of the twenty-first century. The costs, which total € 590 million according to the index of 2011, are divided between the federal government (€ 478 million), the state of Berlin (€ 32 million), and donations gathered for the reconstruction of the historic Baroque facades (€ 80 million). In addition, € 28.5 million are to be raised for the historic reconstruction of the dome, the three inner portals and the portal openings. The Förderverein Berliner Schloss e. V. is highly motivated and committed and has already raised a considerable sum even before construction begins. This high degree of citizen involvement shows how much enthusiasm there is for the Berliner Schloss – Humboldt-Forum among those who take an interest in this future "showcase" of the Federal Republic of Germany.

Palace site hut with sculptures by Andreas Schlüter, 2012

The New Berliner Schloss: The Architecture

Franco Stella

The Berliner Schloss – Humboldt-Forum expands the Museumsinsel (Museum Island) through the addition of another important site for art and science, and returns to the centre of the city its most distinctive building. The rectangular building has three inner courtyards: the existing Schlüterhof and the "newly invented" Schlossforum and Agorahalle courtyards, which are conceived of as town squares in the centre of Berlin. The building combines reconstructed elements of the Baroque palace and the later dome, which are faithful to the originals, and newly constructed elements. In contrast to many historical monuments reconstructed after destruction during World War II, including almost all residential palaces, one of the special features of this building is the large number of new elements.

Within the unity of the construction, each part of the structure remains clearly recognisable: the connection of the new with the old reflects the identity of the various locations rather than an abstract similarity of the formal language. Regarding the "montage" of new and old parts of the structure, it would be more accurate to speak of a "cutting" technique than a "cross fade", which is used for most partial reconstructions. The façades of the reconstructed parts are not superficial scenery but solid constructions that also reflect the substance of the historical façades in depth.

Five new elements have been planned in dialogue with the reconstructed parts:

- In the area of the former palace buildings, the gallery structure of the Belvedere will form the new front facing the Spree. Like the Baroque palace designed by Schlüter this will result in a four-wing complex. Deeply recessed window niches will make the new Spree-façade look like an independent construction, a generous, timeless loggia façade reminiscent of the arcade gallery built here in 1690 by Johann Arnold Nering.
- Near the former Eosanderhof, two row-like and two cube-like structures will form two new squares (the street-like Schlossforum and the naturally illuminated Agorahalle). Together with the reconstructed elements they will complete the adjoining Schlüterhof square. A public passage connects the Schlossforum with the Schlüterhof.

Three sides the Schlüterhof feature reconstructed façades; the fourth side (the site of the structures of the former transverse building) features a newly designed element. The latter's façade is characterised by the stone-bower theme on the lower two storeys and rendered walls of windows, similar to those of the Baroque wings, on the two upper floors. The open passageways through the reconstructed portals I and V connect the Schlüterhof to the city's public space.

Franco Stella, Berliner Schloss – Humboldt-Forum, Schlossforum, rendering, 2013

Franco Stella, Berliner Schloss –
Humboldt-Forum, view from
Unter den Linden, rendering, 2013

The Schlossforum is both a courtyard in the centre of the building and a public square in the middle of the city, as is the Uffizi cortile in Florence, for example. It extends between the reconstructed portals II and IV, which have always served as the entrance and exit to the palace, and it again connects Breite Strasse and Schlossplatz in the south with the Lustgarten and Unter den Linden in the north. The portals and their open passageways assume the function of city gates here, and the architectural design of the new longitudinal façades is reminiscent of an agora or a forum. In this way the ensemble suggests the ideal figure of the piazza.

The Agorahalle is the entrance and reception area of the Humboldt-Forum. Its height and width are determined by the dimensions of the reconstructed Portal III, which was drawn by Johann Friedrich Eosander according to the model of an ancient Roman triumphal arch. The interplay of this figure and the planned loggias on the other three sides of the entrance hall provides this space with the character of a theatre, in which the "triumphal arch" symbolises the stage wall (*scenae frons*) and the "loges" symbolise the audience galleries. In this way the architecture announces the public events that will take place in the entrance hall.

Franco Stella, Berliner Schloss –
Humboldt-Forum, view of the
Belvedere from Rathausbrücke,
rendering, 2013

Franco Stella, Berliner Schloss –
Humboldt-Forum, Schlüterhof,
rendering, 2013

The agora itself extends across the areas generally accessible to the public on the ground floor: around the entrance hall to the staircase, the temporary-exhibition spaces, the auditorium, the multifunctional room and the exhibition of the area's history, around the Schlossforum and Schlüterhof to the lapidarium, the museum shops and cafés. At the subterranean southwestern corner the Archaeological Window reveals the remains of a basement reaching from the Gothic to the early eighteenth century. Departments of the Zentral- und Landesbibliothek Berlin (Central and Regional Library Berlin), the action room of the Humboldt-Labor (Humboldt Laboratory) that is part of the Humboldt-Universität zu Berlin (Humboldt University of Berlin), and the library of non-European art and cultures

that is part of the Staatliche Museen zu Berlin – Preußischer Kulturbesitz (National Museums in Berlin – Prussian Cultural Heritage) are on the first floor. The exhibition rooms of the Ethnologisches Museum (Ethnological Museum) and of the Museum für Asiatische Kunst (Asian Art Museum) are to be housed on the second and third floors. The possibility of a future reconstruction of important staircases and art-historically significant interiors, such as the Schweizersaal and the Paradekammern, remains because disruptive elements in the supporting framework have been avoided. The agora, the Schlossforum and Schlüterhof are three new town squares within the Humboldt-Forum that stand for the unique meaning of this "site of dialogue of world cultures", also as a site of urban life in the heart of the city of Berlin.

Franco Stella, Berliner Schloss – Humboldt-Forum, agora/entrance hall, rendering, 2013

The Humboldt-Forum: From the Parts to the Whole

Martin Heller

The long history of the Humboldt-Forum is a lesson in the democratic formation of will. Even before the details of the architecture and subject matter had been settled, this project dominated the public discussion in Germany. A wide variety of forces and counterforces stimulated and hampered one another both intensely and uncontrollably. Parliamentary power and citizen action came together or remained at odds, until they reached the point when all the often-grotesque quarrels about a suspicion of revanchism, a glorification of history, and colonial guilt faded and made visible and tangible the uniqueness that distinguishes the Humboldt-Forum and that now fascinates an ever-growing circle of people.

Wherein does this uniqueness lie? The response to such a key question is – does this really surprise anyone? – as simple as it is complicated. The Humboldt-Forum is unique because it manifests – in the heart of the German capital, as it were – a strong claim to cosmopolitanism and a willingness to learn that, given the ideological and political significance of the project, has to be upheld if the Federal Republic as its patron is to avoid damaging its own reputation. This realisation brings us immediately to the complex discussion and analysis of all the factors that have to interact to ensure that this new institution functions successfully.

These factors can be identified and discussed. But from the start the success of the Humboldt-Forum depends on two qualities that have already been binding guidelines during its development. Firstly, it is necessary to produce from many individual motivations and interests a totality in which the participating partners know they are united for a common goal and adapt their actions to one another. And secondly, we must avow the presence and contemporaneity of perception and thinking, which will no doubt derive unsuspected energy from the reconstruction of the Berliner Schloss (Berlin Palace) now in progress.

A present totality

Why this presence and why a totality? Because the Humboldt-Forum is not simply a particularly elaborate museum for non-European arts and cultures that will also house several libraries, the knowledge platform of a university, and a diverse programme of events. That conception is far too simplistic. The new institution seeks to turn mere cohabitation into coexistence by establishing shared, binding objectives for all participants as

Dahlem Goes to Town: Aztec sun disc, Ethnologisches Museum, at the Friedrichstrasse railway station

Dahlem Goes to Town: Indian Krishna figure, Museum für Asiatische Kunst, at the Friedrichstrasse railway station

well as a framework for action in which individual strengths can be brought to bear as a coherent overall profile. Cooperating with and taking advantage of one another in this way will generate added value that has scarcely been imaginable until now. To that end, the future Humboldt-Forum will need a self-image that responds to the opportunity to adapt, expand and rearrange existing approaches to and traditions for the subject matter. And it needs a sense not only for the topicality of questions and themes but also for how they are treated and imparted in a form indebted to its own time.

Characteristically, for a long time during the planning of the Humboldt-Forum there was a special, albeit ill-defined area that was intended to manifest and guarantee such commonality and such presence in exemplary fashion with an authority borrowed from Greek antiquity: the agora. As a space for events on the ground floor, the agora was designed with various semi-public and public rooms for temporary events and pro-grammes: the entrance hall, an auditorium, a room with a stage, two large exhibition spaces, a repertory cinema and the open Schlüterhof courtyard, as well as food services and stores. These offerings will be supplemented by a constant survey of the history of the site, an Archaeological Window, and a prominent reference to the formal art collection of the Berliner Schloss.

This mixture and its sense of being a living place of exchange seemed to many of those who joined in the discussions of the development of the Humboldt-Forum to be the true core task being set for this politically grounded institution. It was to be a place where pointed thematic work on Germany and the world would come together; where the sciences and arts would cause us to forget all barriers; where culture on the highest level would become tangible and comprehensible for everyone. This ambition was under-standable, but it was neither justified nor achievable, at least not with the idealistic abso-luteness that during the debates about the architecture and conception of the Humboldt-Forum regarded the agora as a bulwark with universal attraction. The agora alone was expected to ensure that culture was able to transcend even the façades of the Prussian palace – which were disliked by many – and establish the good, true and correct in its interior.

Nevertheless, the higher the ideals were stacked up, the more the discourse about the agora became uncoupled from the reality of planning the Humboldt-Forum. Hence this common desire turned out not to be a cure but rather more like a constant wound whose bleeding could not be stanched. All the provisions regarding the process of construction now finally had to articulate the subject matter more concisely; they could be fomented or parried by reference to the theses about the agora that were circulating, but not truly addressed. And something else emerged: the claim to the present and to presence cannot be delegated for the whole to parts of this unique cultural site without costs. It applies to all. The events area, whose effects are directed largely outward; the knowledge workshops of the libraries on the second floor; the rich cosmos of the two museum floors – all of these things contribute to the desire to be anchored in the here and now and will pursue it so as not to diminish the significance and influence of such ideas.

At this point a redefinition – of the concept and of the thing – became inevitable. The agora as a territorial sphere was replaced by the idea of an agora as substance, and that altered work at the Humboldt-Forum as a whole. The transparency of the participating institutions, actors, arguments and images has been called for ever since – in competition and coordination but also in justified distinction.

Increasingly, the Humboldt-Forum thus appears to be a highly differentiated clockwork mechanism or even an organism with components that mesh precisely, whose interplay as a whole accounts for the particularity that can do justice to the presence in the first place. At the same time, there is a growing awareness that all the ideas definitely need to be made more concrete, and that the era of merely theoretical or even rhetorical demands on the content and influence is over.

Working toward a practice

But what does it mean in this context to make things more concrete? First of all, nothing other than the constant testing of all ideas against what the Humboldt-Forum is as a place: a building with rooms, natural lighting, pathways, moods, acoustic qualities, prospects, strengths and weaknesses. At the same time, however, this building is more: it is a piece of reconstructed history, the recreation of a starting point that had disappeared, a democratic palace. All of this was, of course, not yet tangible at the time of the cornerstone ceremony but rather has to be constantly imagined, with the help of plans, renderings, descriptions, suppositions. In a complicated way, that which does not yet exist begins to emerge, along with what it is supposed to refer to explicitly.

To cite just one example, one that will take up two entire floors of the finished Humboldt-Forum: Such complication should be expected, among other things, when those responsible for the museum work with exhibition designers to develop new solutions for presenting their collections. For decades many of these objects had their fixed place in Dahlem in the context of arrangements that had been developed on the basis of clearly different assumptions – namely, from an understanding that we can only comprehend in a limited way today for what their foreignness means for us as viewers, with other scholarly approaches, in other spaces, and for a different audience. It is always difficult to break free from what seem to be foregone conclusions. That had consequences for the process of planning the move from Dahlem to Berlin-Mitte in that the construction of the new was a long-term and continuous process. There are more or less precise desires as to what should be expressed in the museum exhibitions of the Humboldt-Forum when it comes to current theoretical findings. And similarly there is above all the understandable and welcome desire to transgress one's own boundaries and surprise oneself with discoveries.

Once again: it is not a simple matter to make this reality. The new demands favourable circumstances, needs a climate of incentive, needs inspirations, comparisons, even mistakes and dead ends. That is the only way to outwit the tenaciousness of the habitual, which often enough we are not even aware of, because it knows how to sell itself as professional confidence and mastery or as an inevitable practical necessity. The price of the new is that something that seems to be a solid aspect of one's own identity has to be made fluid.

The laboratory as model

Under that motto, work at the Humboldt Lab Dahlem began in spring 2012. This work, which is scheduled and budgeted to take four years, is now part of the central preparations for the operation of the Humboldt-Forum, and its first results have already revealed the fruitful dynamic such a project can trigger. What does this laboratory aim to achieve? What exactly does it have to do with the Humboldt-Forum, and how will it open up the necessary latitude between utility and experiment?

The idea of the Humboldt Lab Dahlem arose from an assessment that was as obvious as it was banal: Innovation cannot be pulled out of a hat. Once again: anyone who wants to create something new needs time and the opportunity to experiment. The lab is intended to guarantee both. As a kind of experimental stage for everyone familiar with the task, the collections of the Ethnologisches Museum (Ethnological Museum) and the Museum für Asiatische Kunst (Asian Art Museum) will be reinstalled on two floors of the Humboldt-Forum.

This task is a difficult one. Just taking a walk through the permanent exhibitions in Dahlem will suffice to appreciate the high artistic and cultural qualities that have been assembled, studied, and exhibited here for decades. To present them in a new way at the Humboldt-Forum thus means doing justice to this quality while at the same time redefining, understanding and dramatising the topicality of all the non-European objects. For although it is still a construction site and there is no building yet, it is already certain: The Humboldt-Forum will be anything but a traditional museum institution. Its target is to conquer new territory in many respects, and it wants to and will confront the present. The nearly sixteen thousand square metres the two museums moving from Dahlem will occupy form part of an even more impressive totality, and this totality is seeking – for now as a goal and not yet a reality – a dramaturgy conceived and shaped as a whole.

To return to the Humboldt Lab Dahlem: although every attempt to describe it immediately leads to pathos-laden exaggeration, we have to bring it down to earth so that

its seed can germinate. The lab is a programme that attempts to solve problems of representation in an exemplary, clear, and forward-looking way. This happens under the eyes of the interested public by setting tasks for which museums often lack the money, time and energy. The experiments of the lab are thus practical in orientation. They must and will bear fruit for the planning of the museum world at the Humboldt-Forum. The two processes relate to each other like a support leg and a free leg: The support leg does the work and the free leg facilitates far-reaching eccentrics but without reducing every stance or gait to heavy-handed awkwardness. But both legs are aware that they belong to the same body, and their coordination is assured by harmonising the organization of the lab and the museum planning.

The exemplary nature of the Humboldt Lab Dahlem is demonstrated even beyond its methodological vocation proper. For example, it provides other museums with illustrations of how they can work with the worlds of historical objects in contemporary ways, and it even contributes on a high level to the discussion of suitable scenography for them. At the same time, however, the lab turns out to be a model for the Humboldt-Forum itself. What happens there, in a calculated dovetailing of testing and planning for both museums, will continue to be pursued in a focused way, in an attempt to bring together users, especially those who do not belong to an institution, and to put them into play,

Dahlem Goes to Town: Columbian death mask, Ethnologisches Museum, on Alexanderplatz literally, in the new facility. If this model was adopted and interpreted with appropriate freedom, the planning process would have the opportunity to do justice to its own challenges.

Building up and rehearsing!

From this perspective it becomes completely clear which factors have to come together at the Humboldt-Forum in order for it not only to complete its task but also to continue to operate, in a constant effort to follow the path of global objects attentively and make them its theme. For: the proper spectrum of themes for the events and other offerings is no more sufficient in itself than adequate financing, professionalism of events, or restraint in civil society and politics would be. All of these things are indispensable and must be achieved. The totality of the Humboldt-Forum needs a series of special sensitivities and competencies both internal and external, that have to be built up and rehearsed in the coming years.

Above all, that means a great deal of trust. Internally, among the users who participate: they are already invited to approach one another unconditionally in order to agree on their goals and opportunities but also to work together to expand them. In addition

Dahlem Goes to Town: Chinese gong, Ethnologisches Museum, at the construction site of the Berliner Schloss – Humboldt-Forum

to the building of the Humboldt-Forum proper, it is necessary to cooperate carefully on planning with an eye to its own demands as a library or a cinema. All the relationships that result in this way have to be subject to certain tests of resilience if the work itself is to be viable.

This trust is not just needed for the subject matter and concept in the spirit of the Humboldt Lab Dahlem; it also needs an operational framework that has to be constructed piece by piece on the basis of a plan that brings the mobility and controllability of the new institution, whose enormous scale predictably presents a number of problems of management, into a suitable organisational concept. We need to strive for artistic direction in the sense of an approach to work and a responsibility that are essentially determined by the concerns of the arts and the content. And we need the flexibility for the Humboldt-Forum to react at short notice to the international social and cultural movements we encounter daily. Like every concept, this calls for appropriate planning, and so the years available to us have to be used to the best of our abilities to achieve that goal.

Part of the image of the slowly emerging totality is the necessity to establish a tight-knit, worldwide network of partnerships. The existing connections of all the users of the Humboldt-Forum provide a welcome foundation for that. Here too the networks have to be re-examined and reinforced in terms of their content: The Humboldt-Forum has to establish and live an attitude that enables its partners to participate truly – even beyond scholarly exchange, generosity when loaning objects, and treating one another fairly – in the adventure of the new that is starting in Berlin and that will seek answers from there.

One last thing: The Humboldt-Forum has to get to know its audience. Not just its target audience – marketing criteria are important but are not everything – but also the audience to which it owes its existence and its legitimacy and with which it wants to share and move the world. This audience lives in Berlin and everywhere else. It expects a lot of the Humboldt-Forum, and rightly so, but it also offers it a lot: interest, attention, and the everyday knowledge and feeling that no institution, with all its conflicting interests, can create itself.

Moreover, this audience and its world stand for what the history of the Humboldt-Forum thus far has been aiming for: for the Berliner Schloss, in which culture and democracy will replace the former centre of monarchic power. It is no longer the presumption of an individual that holds this totality together. The democratic palace, made possible and supported by democratic institutions, will only do justice to its ambition if it feels its obligation to everyone. Everyone who seeks in the palace the mirror and the motivation for what preoccupies them – with a playful enthusiasm that is one of the most beautiful and valuable things that the Humboldt-Forum can make its own.

Making an Impact:
From Royal Palace to Modern
International Cultural Centre

The Humboldt-Forum welcomes visitors on the ground floor with a wide range of attractions. The entrance hall functions as the centre of gravity. Here the dimensions of the historical palace cannot fail to impress the visitor; a lively, bustling atmosphere prevails as tickets and information are obtained, while display screens provide visitors with a foretaste of the events and discoveries to be found inside the Humboldt-Forum. The objects and installations in the encircling galleries of the upper floors evoke the historical Kunstkammer (cabinet of art and curiosities) of the past and testify to the perpetual inquisitiveness of humans in solving the world's riddles. The entrance hall also houses an exhibition, freely accessible to everyone, describing the colourful history of the site. Organised by the Stiftung Berliner Schloss – Humboldtforum (Berlin Palace – Humboldtforum Foundation), the show will illustrate – together with the Archaeological Window and the Lapidarium – the path from the first palace buildings to the present-day Humboldt-Forum.

The first floor is primarily an attractive event area. An arthouse cinema, an auditorium for music, dance and performance art, rooms for special exhibitions, and the spacious Schlüterhof courtyard are the venues for an expansive and internationally-oriented cultural centre. This is where the Humboldt-Forum realises its aspirations of not only transmitting a contemporary understanding of our globalised world, but also of making clear the economical and ecological trends in world society and indicating which tasks lie before us in the spheres of politics, business and society when tackling them. The guiding principle is a mixture of entertainment, committed thematic formats and repeatedly displayed artistic positions, which result in a stimulating public meeting place, a forum for all and a marketplace for many things. This also includes a public commercial zone around the Schlüterhof, concentrating restaurants and shops and guaranteeing quality in this respect as well.

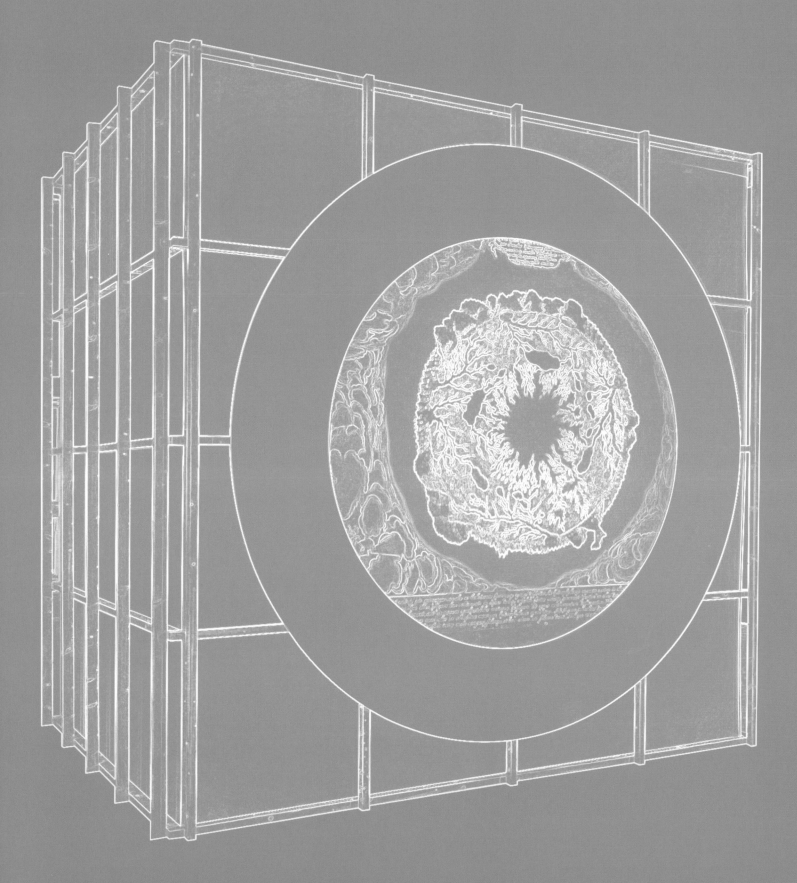

Horst Bredekamp/Michael Eissenhauer

The Kunstkammer
as Nucleus

In the spring of 1700 the great philosopher, mathematician and natural scientist Gottfried Wilhelm Leibniz sent a memorandum to the Elector of Brandenburg, Frederick III. In it he attempted to explain why a "Society" of scholars, similar to the academies of science that had already existed for decades in Paris and London, would be indispensable for Prussia if the state did not want to fall hopelessly behind. With respect to the provision of such a society, which was to be located in Berlin, he mentioned a series of facilities, apart from a library, which from today's perspective hardly seem to have anything to do with an academy of science: "libraries of images (or collections of prints, drawings, statues and paintings), cabinets of art and rarities, armouries, gardens of many kinds, as well as vivaria and the great works of nature and art, of which your Serene Highness has no shortage, for a theatre of nature and art."

Leibniz had by this time already been pursing the project of "a theatre of nature and art" for three decades. He formulated his ideas for it in a particularly forceful and witty manner in a text published in 1675 in Paris, *Drôle de Pensée, touchant une nouvelle sorte de représentations* (Funny Thoughts, Regarding a New Kind of Representation). Starting from contemporary attempts to walk on the waters of the Seine or to levitate in the air by means of apparatuses (fig. p. 53), Leibniz listed a variety of collections and research, entertainment and educational institutions. Aside from cabinets of art and curiosities, he mentioned observatories, botanical gardens, anatomical theatres and menageries, but also technical museums and event venues. This institutionally-connected complex of a *Theatrum Naturae et Artis* was to form part of the provision of an academy of science. The development of this "new kind of representation" relied on a playful approach and enjoyment of amazing phenomena. A varied mise-en-scène aimed to stimulate the cognitive abilities of humans as well as their perceptual capabilities and imagination. In this sense, Leibniz's ideas proposed a profound reform of the sciences following the principal metaphor of the theatre.

In Berlin the Kunstkammer (cabinet of art and curiosities) of the Electoral Palace offered Leibniz a new source of inspiration for his considerations. Such collections were usually arranged along the lines of objects from nature, the arts and the sciences, that is, *naturalia, artificialia,* and *scientifica.* The Berlin Kunstkammer was likewise characterised by this classification scheme; its emphasis, however, lay on the area of *artificialia* and this was to define its character through all of its future transformations.

Samuel Blesendorf, Ideal View of a Room of the Cabinet of Antiquities in the Royal Palace in Berlin, from: Lorenz Beger, *Thesaurus Brandenburgicus,* 1696, I, before p. 1

page 51
Anton Mozart, The Presentation of the Pomeranian Cabinet of Curiosities to Duke Philip II of Pomerania, 1615/16 (detail)

This is all the more remarkable as the Berlin Kunstkammer had been destroyed to a large extent during the Thirty Years' War, so that it had to be founded anew by the Great Elector, Frederick William of Brandenburg, in the middle of the seventeenth century. His preferences were for non-European artefacts, principally from Asia, Africa and Brazil, as well as for coins, medals, antique sculptures and artworks of the post-antiquity period. These tendencies were accompanied by an interest in exploring the natural history of the world, not simply limited to malformations and similar "natural wonders", but also extending to the exemplary investigation of the natural riches as well as the flora and fauna of his territory.

The rapidly growing number of items in the Kunstkammer led to a continual alternation between the spin-off of individual categories and the strengthening of the comprehensive nature of the Kunstkammer. Thus the antiquities and coin sections, for example, were separated off in 1686, but the Pomeranian Art Cabinet by Philipp Hainhofer was added to the collection in 1689, once more manifesting the universal aspirations of the Kunstkammer (fig. p. 51). Itself a miniature Kunstkammer collection, this luxurious large cabinet was unified by a multifaceted exploration of the world: It ranged from measuring and drawing devices to tableware and toiletry articles, tools and games. The cabinet was destroyed by fire in World War II, but the majority of the over 200 objects preserved in it have survived. Just like many of the other items from the former Kunstkammer they belong today to the collection of the Kunstgewerbemuseum (Museum of Decorative Arts) of the Staatliche Museen zu Berlin (National Museums in Berlin).

Around 1700 the collection had once more grown to such an extent that it could claim nine prestigious rooms on the fourth floor of the newly erected palace by Andreas Schlüter (fig. p. 52). For Leibniz the Kunstkammer was a place where all-encompassing researching and collecting, entertainment, playing and learning, exhibiting and presenting could be carried out. In his eyes its complex arrangement harboured almost utopian possibilities. Yet his endeavours to expand the Kunstkammer and the academy into a "theatre of nature and art", which he pursued until the end of his life, were only partially successful. Alone the cost of the royal coronation of 1701 and the subsequent expenses put an end to all prospects of a generous financing of the Berlin Scientific Society.

It was only in 1797, when the Kunstkammer had reached a precarious status after decades of neglect and the removal of parts of the collection, that it once again become the centre of attention. After Frederick William III had acceded to the throne, he attempted to inject new substance into the similarly languishing Academy of Science. One of his measures consisted of placing the royal library and the Kunstkammer under the control of the Academy. The collections remained in the care of the head of the Kunstkammer, Jean Henry. He was able to bring the collections of antique sculpture and coins back to the palace from Potsdam, whither they had been moved. Together with the large section of non-European objects and the artefacts of North European prehistory, Henry had such an extensive collection that the rooms available on the mezzanine level of the palace were no longer sufficient. In 1805 Henry proposed erecting a royal museum of natural history and art, which would transform the Kunstkammer into a universal museum which would thereby be created.

This suggestion was taken up in 1807 by Alexander von Humboldt. His concept, the importance of which it is impossible to overestimate, called for all the collections located in Berlin to be united under the umbrella of the Academy of Science. This venture of founding a universal museum, for which the Kunstkammer would constitute the back-

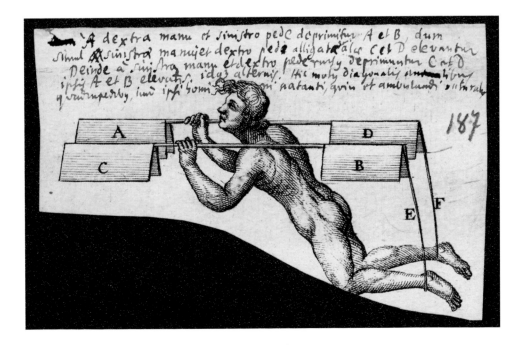

Flight attempt of the locksmith Besnier, supplement to: Gottfried Wilhelm Leibniz, *Drôle de Pensée*, 1675

bone, was the key to the subsequent history of museology in Berlin. Two years later this idea was combined with the scheme of founding a university in Berlin, a project supported by Wilhelm von Humboldt and a group of fellow campaigners. In 1810 a royal decree had the mineralogical, zoological and anatomical display objects from the palace transferred to the newly founded university and united there with the private collections of researchers and of institutions such as the Mining Academy. Only the ground floor in the east wing of the university building was designated for classrooms; the rest, that is, five sixths of the entire building, was intended for the medical and natural science collections as well as for the picture gallery and the gems and coins cabinet. This is where the Giustiniani collection of paintings, purchased by Frederick William III in 1815, was displayed and added to, forming the nucleus of the Berlin Gemäldegalerie (Old Master Paintings). Until the inauguration in 1830 of Karl Friedrich Schinkel's Royal Museum, the present-day Altes Museum, the university once more expressed the comprehensive concept of the Kunstkammer. And Schinkel's museum also profited from the early collecting activity for the Kunstkammer by accepting its antiquities, paintings, and sculptures.

The objects of art and decorative art remaining in the palace were extensively described in 1838 by the art historian Franz Kugler. In the prologue to this publication he referred to the ethnological objects , which had been growing continually during the previous decades, and at least summarily highlighted the wealth of this collection. His *Handbuch der Kunstgeschichte* (Handbook of Art History), published in 1842, the first truly universal history of art, was based on the objects in the Kunstkammer. Kugler compared all of the world's visual cultures without placing undue emphasis on the prestige of the Mediter-

Karl Friedrich Schinkel,
Ground plan of the Kunstkammer
in the Berliner Schloss, 1838

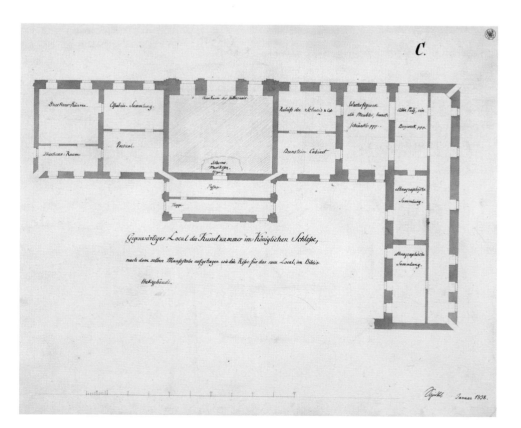

Entrance hall in the Humboldt-Forum
(film still), design FOCUS + ECHO,
Andreas Pinkow, 2013

ranean cultures. He thus acknowledged the genuine art historical value of sculptures from Mexico when he described these as "equivalent to the best works of Egyptian art".

A ground plan by Karl Friedrich Schinkel (fig. p. 54) from 1838 informs us of the purpose of the individual rooms, in part determined by tradition and in part newly designated: to the left the director's rooms and the foyer, with the ivory collection adjacent; the Amber Cabinet and the Room of Geographic Reliefs is located to the right of the Knight's Hall; next to them were several rooms with wax figures, furniture and fine cabinets, items of clothing, and the model of a mine; and finally the two large rooms of the ethnological collection. Kugler's description of the works in the Kunstkammer and Schinkel's ground plan depicted a collection whose space was available for re-assignment only shortly afterwards. In 1843 construction of the Neues Museum began according to plans by Friedrich August Stüler. During the course of the 1850s the gradual consolidation of the Egyptian, Greek-Roman and Northern European antiquities collections, the ethnological works, the collection of plaster casts of sculpture from around the world and the cabinet of prints, together with the art and decorative art objects from the palace, formed a highly modern version of the Kunstkammer, defending and focusing the character of the Kunstkammer in a grand style that encompassed the entire world and created a true microcosm.

This miscellaneous collection continued to exist until the 1880s, when the decorative art objects were moved to the Kunstgewerbemuseum built by Martin Gropius and Heino Schmieden and the ethnological collections to the neighbouring Königliches Museum für Völkerkunde (Royal Museum of Ethnology). The natural science collections of the university, likewise rooted in the Kunstkammer, had by this time similarly grown out of all proportion; they were then transferred in 1889 to the newly founded Museum für Naturkunde (Museum of Natural History).

The unique character of Berlin's museum history in the nineteenth century is marked by the contradictory interaction of diverging positions. Wilhelm von Humboldt, if one wants to personalise these antagonisms, aimed at a liberation of the aesthetic energy of the objects from all aristocratic, instrumental, and pedagogic ownership. In contrast, Alexander von Humboldt saw the museum as an organ of reflection on a universal scale, in a tradition ultimately reaching back to Leibniz. Both concepts, which found expression in the contrasting configurations of the Altes Museum and Neues Museum, are wonderful and both concepts mutually support each other in their contrasting approaches. The history of the Berlin museums evolved within the luxury of this conflict.

The historiography of European museums customarily regards the change from the eighteenth to the nineteenth century as a turning point, when specialised museums replaced the universal Kunstkammer. Yet the uninterrupted history of its objects demonstrates that the Berlin Kunstkammer can not only be considered the nucleus of the exceptionally rich Berlin museums in all areas of knowledge and collecting, but that it set an example well into a period when according to the categories of traditional museum history it should have long become obsolete. By committing itself to the idea of being both a collection and a research laboratory, the Humboldt-Forum continues a tradition that ever since its first formulation in the sixteenth century has remained a constant aspiration throughout all of its transformations.

Gottfried Wilhelm Leibniz thought in horizons that modernity has painfully lost through the sharp separation of the different spheres of knowledge and collecting. Invoking him today, as has already been attempted in the framework of the Humboldt Lab in Dahlem (fig. p. 57), does not mean, however, cosily bringing together again the divided spheres in the sense of a diffuse holism. Instead, the diversified areas are to be juxtaposed in a stimulating situation of tension, in order to enable the interplay of objects that encounter one another on the plateau of the collections to "converse" with one another, and to trigger associations. As the interdisciplinary association of three major educational institutions, the Humboldt-Forum can make the desire of the great Leibniz come true and function equally as an archive, think tank, laboratory and stage.

Humboldt Lab Dahlem, Probebühne 1 (Rehearsal Stage 1), Project Gedanken-scherz (Funny Thoughts), March 2013

Reconstructing the Kunstkammer itself in its physical state or even filling it with the display objects is neither possible nor desirable. Instead, its memory is to be brought alive in the Humboldt-Forum's entrance hall, whose extension and position provide the space to do justice to the concept and to its *longue durée*. The entrance hall is the centrepiece of the entire building. A roofed public meeting place will arise here and will welcome guests and prepare them for a varied journey of experience and discovery. The encircling galleries offer the space for a mise-en-scène across three floors, in which objects, media and visual installations will continue the principles of the former Kunstkammer. Developments in the history of ideas reaching up until the present will be taken up and linked with one another associatively in thematically-grouped niches. A comprehensive lighting concept will expand the entrance hall into a stereogram, composed of light and movement, turning the niches and galleries into a platform for the appropriation of the world (fig. p. 55). Instead of a linear narrative within a closed room, the dynamic potential of the Kunstkammer will be experienced in a contemporary paraphrase. A modern theatre of knowledge will arise in this manner from the nucleus of the Kunstkammer, one that invites visitors to explore the concept of the Humboldt-Forum and its humanistic dimensions in an intuitive and playful, as well as a systematic, manner.

Bernhard Wolter

The Berliner Schloss as an Obligation: On the History of the Site of Germany's Most Prominent Cultural Building Project

The Humboldt-Forum within the reconstructed Baroque façades of the former royal palace will revive a site in the heart of Germany's capital that is steeped in history and that has marked the city for more than 500 years. The construction of the Berliner Schloss (Berlin Palace) harks back to a time when the small twin towns of Berlin-Cölln, with their unpaved roads, wooden huts, and a small number of churches and monasteries, made a very humble impression. Elector Frederick II laid the foundation stone here in 1443 for a fortress to support his claim to power in the Margravate of Brandenburg beyond his residence in Brandenburg on the Havel, marking the start of the reign of the Hohenzollern dynasty in Berlin and Cölln.

We do not really know what that first fortress on the Spree looked like, since little of the building remains. Surviving drawings and paintings show only the new Renaissance palace erected by Elector Joachim II some 100 years later. With its imposing new wing with 13 window axes facing the Schlossplatz and perpendicular to the Spree, the castle underscored the political significance of the House of Brandenburg within the Empire. The Berliner Schloss confirms Wolf Jobst Siedler's central thesis that – in contrast to other European capitals – the royal palace in Berlin existed before the city and that the city could not have developed without the palace: "The palace was not located in Berlin. Berlin was the palace." This building on its central site defined the city's appearance and development from almost the very beginning.

The four main phases of its complicated architectural history can only be briefly mentioned here. Initially, Elector Frederick III commissioned Andreas Schlüter, sculptor and director of palace building, with the transformation of the old Renaissance castle into a Baroque royal palace in 1699. Frederick was thus able to move into his new residence in Berlin in triumph after returning to Prussia from Königsberg as King Frederick I in May 1701.

page 59
View over the Kupfergraben canal of the west façade of the Berliner Schloss with the Eosanderportal, ca. 1910

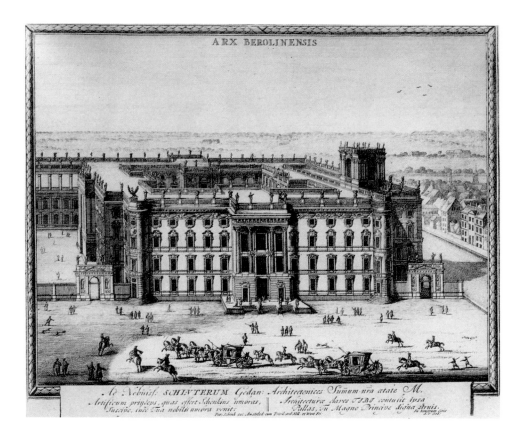

J. U. Krauss, Perspective view of the Berliner Schloss, 1701

View from the Schlossplatz to the ruins of the Berliner Schloss, May 1945

The palace was not actually finished as a true residence until 1716 under his considerably more frugal successor, the "Soldier-King" Frederick William I, first by the architect Johann Friedrich Eosander, then by Martin Heinrich Böhme. From then onwards the palace remained outwardly unchanged for almost 150 years; the interior, however, was energetically furnished and rebuilt. The imposing dome over the large Roman triumphal arch of the Eosanderportal (Portal III) on the west façade was planned under Frederick William IV while he was still a crown prince; he designed it together with Karl Friedrich Schinkel, and it was completed by 1853 by the latter's disciple Friedrich August Stüler. Today it is hard to imagine the palace without its dome, which raises interesting questions about the current reconstruction planning. Should the façades be broken up by the small Baroque window divisions or by the larger windows with muntins from the nineteenth century? The Foundation Board has recently decided this question in favour of the larger window panes by referring to the dome – in particular as the smaller panes were not a design choice but were conditioned by the limited technical possibilities in Prussia in the early eighteenth century.

At the end of the nineteenth century another essential transformation took place that affected the surroundings rather than the palace itself. Emperor William II had the row of houses of the so-called Schlossfreiheit opposite the Eosanderportal razed in 1894 to make room for the national monument to Emperor William I. This opened up the view of the palace from Unter den Linden, while the Lustgarten side gained importance compared to the open square of the Schlossplatz. The history of the site naturally also includes the heavy damage suffered during the last months of World War II in the winter of 1944-45, the building's use as an exhibition venue, although a ruin, in 1946, and the complete demolition by order of Walter Ulbricht in 1950. Ultimately, Schlossplatz was renamed Marx-Engels-Platz and became the parade ground for the May Day demonstrations, with a large stand erected along the River Spree to view them. Construction of the Palast der Republik (Palace of the Rebublic) began 25 years later. Together with the State Council Building in the south and the GDR Foreign Ministry on the opposite side of the Spree branch in the west, the Palast der Republik formed the central state forum of the GDR. The resurrection of the Berliner Schloss as the Humboldt-Forum will turn the Prussian royal residence into a public building in the best sense of the word, a place in the centre of the city where its citizens and the city itself can regain their identity at the cultural level of the twenty-first century.

On the ground floor the Stiftung Berliner Schloss – Humboldtforum (Berlin Palace – Humboldtforum Foundation) will set up its own exhibition on the long, turbulent history of the site. The royal palace was the home of the electors of Brandenburg, the kings of Prussia and the emperors of Germany. The November Revolution, the abdication of the emperor in 1918, the palace as museum during the Weimar Republic, the burnt-out war ruin, the razing of the palace, the Palast der Republik and its dismantling due to the hazards posed by asbestos – all of these events will be dealt with here. The remains of the cellars with the Baroque cellar vaults, uncovered during recent excavations, the palace commander's former guardhouse, and the blast holes from 1950, will be accessible to visitors in the Archaeological Window. In this manner visitors will be able to step directly into the history of the site.

Exhibition on the history of the site, design of room arrangement, FOCUS + ECHO, Andreas Pinkow, 2013

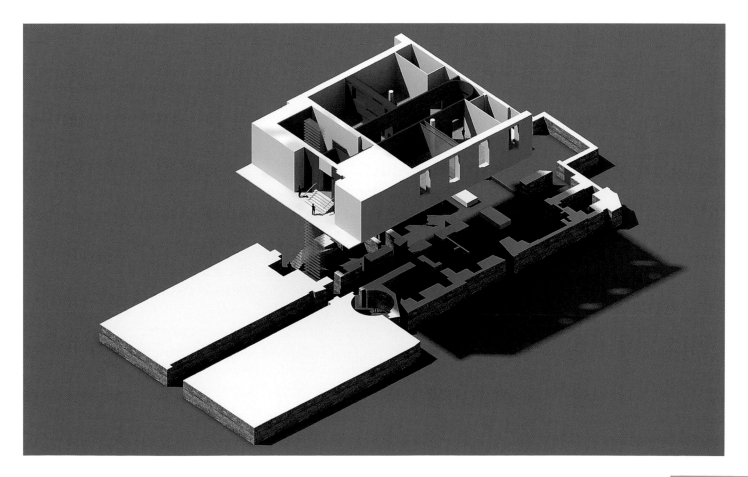

Matthias Wemhoff

The Cellars of the Berliner Schloss, or Bringing the Underground to Light: On the Origins of the Archaeological Window

The exposure of the cellars at the northwest corner of the Berliner Schloss (Berlin Palace) represents the start of the long path that ultimately led to the decision to reconstruct the palace as the Humboldt-Forum. On the initiative of the Förderverein Berliner Schloss e. V. (Association Berliner Schloss) the cellars at the northwest corner were excavated as visible evidence of the palace. These cellars, however, fulfilled only a substitute function for a long time, evoking the palace and ultimately promoting the reconstruction of its façades. The value of the cellars themselves as the last remaining authentic foundations of the palace on the site was not recognised for a long time. For more than ten years they lay exposed to the elements without any protection. And when the architectural competition for the building of the Humboldt-Forum was ultimately tendered, the preservation of the cellars was only an option and not a condition.

At this point in 2009 the Berliner Landesdenkmalamt (Berlin Monument Authority) had already begun to excavate other cellars in the southwest corner systematically. The construction of the GDR Palast der Republik (Palace of the Republic) had destroyed the entire archaeological substance in the eastern half of the site of the palace. This made the careful excavation of the remaining areas all the more important. It quickly became apparent that the cellars south of the Eosanderportal were particularly well preserved. It seemed unimaginable that these original remnants of the palace should make way for a building that had essentially arisen from the desire to reconstruct the lost substance, at least as regards the façades. An international conference, "The underground city – urban archaeology and inner city development in Europe", held that same year framed the situation in Berlin within an international context; it demonstrated that the preservation, integration and revitalisation of archaeological remains had currently become a key task for

Archaeological Window,
Design proposal, FOCUS + ECHO,
Andreas Pinkow, 2013

page 63
Cellar under the Eosanderportal
with detonation craters from 1950

preservation experts and city planners. The conference closed with the declaration of the "Berlin Agenda", explicitly calling for "the development of creative architectural, technical and communicative solutions allowing Berlin's citizens and visitors access to the original remnants of the palace and its surrounding structures".

Franco Stella placed great value on the preservation of the cellars in his proposal. Based on his planning and thanks to wide-ranging public support, a constructive dialogue was soon initiated with the building's clients and planners, leading to the decision to preserve the cellars south of the Eosanderportal and to make them accessible to the public. These cellars offer a good insight into all the various phases of use of the palace across the centuries. For this reason, the planning took into consideration the access and guidance of visitors from the beginning. The entrance area directly at the Eosanderportal leads downwards to the cellar level. The cellars have for the most part been left in the state in which they were found during the excavation. The new building, however, naturally has to have foundations. Six concrete columns will be carefully inserted into this cellar area and – it remains to be hoped – will not intervene in the historical substance any more than necessary.

The experience of the walls and floors, so heavily marked by history, will be the main experience of the circuit through the Archaeological Window. High-quality lighting, which directs the gaze to the walls and the floor and allows the modern concrete ceiling to recede into the background, is therefore vital for the corresponding effect. At the beginning the viewer will see a long passage under the Eosanderportal. Here the massiveness of the Baroque walls will be contrasted with the pits and destruction left behind by the blasting operations during the demolition. Visitors will walk through several well-preserved Baroque rooms, in which individual finds from the excavation will be displayed in a thematic context. In the middle of the circuit there is a large area deeper than the cellar, created by the building of a massive district heating pipe. It now offers an ideal place to present the finds from the former Berliner Schloss together with a documentation of the destruction during the war and the ensuing demolition.

Another path leads alongside structures added during the Wilhelmine period to the oldest masonry and thus somewhat further than the south wall of the palace. During construction at the beginning of the eighteenth century parts of the northern wing of the former Dominican monastery erected around 1300 were integrated into the new building. The Gothic brickwork thus links the palace with the city's history. The path to the exit leads the visitor between the new and the old foundations of the exterior wall of the palace's wing and transmits the exciting contrast between past and present. For the former royal palace has not disappeared without trace. Parts of the cellar level have survived under Schlossplatz. In future we shall be able to walk through original rooms in the Archaeological Window that prove that the new façade and the entire building indeed stand precisely on the correct site.

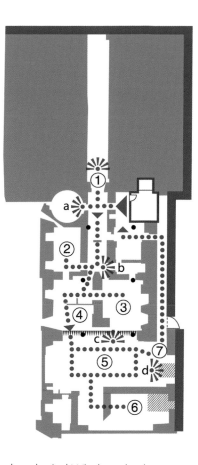

Archaeological Window circuit:
1. Passage under the Eosanderportal,
2. Museum objects from the war ruins, 3. Guardroom of the palace commander, 4. Furnaces and heating,
5. Bomb attack and demolition,
6. City, monastery, and palace,
7. Exterior views; a. Basement of tower staircase, b. Corridor with stairs, c. Floors from three centuries, d. District heating pipes

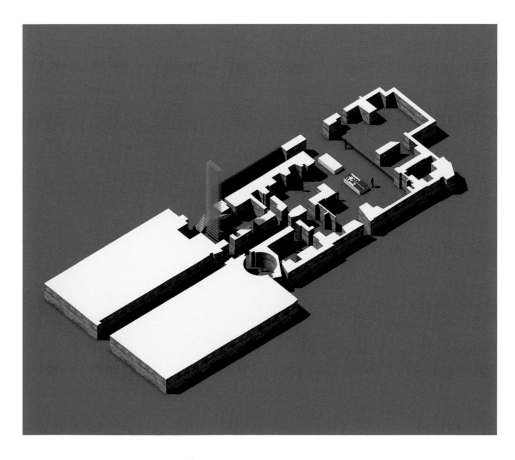

Archaeological Window, Proposal for rooms, FOCUS + ECHO, Andreas Pinkow, 2013

Pointing the Way:
World of Languages,
Display Window of Research,
Workshops of Knowledge

The First Floor brings together the three institutions constituting the Humboldt-Forum: the Stiftung Preußischer Kulturbesitz (Prussian Cultural Heritage Foundation) with its Staatliche Museen zu Berlin (National Museums in Berlin), the Zentral- und Landesbibliothek Berlin (Central and Regional Library Berlin), and the Humboldt-Universität zu Berlin (Humboldt University of Berlin). Here it becomes clear that the Humboldt-Forum's concept is not only justified by the history of the institutions, whose shared roots as museums, library, and university lie in the Brandenburg-Prussian Kunstkammer (cabinet of art and curiosities) of the Berliner Schloss (Berlin Palace), but that it is also defined by their future missions.

New forms of complementary interaction will thus arise, opening access to an understanding of the world beyond the boundaries of traditional disciplines, true to the legacy of Wilhelm and Alexander von Humboldt. The arts and sciences will enter into a dialogue; knowledge will be made available to all in a modern and comprehensive manner. Distances will be bridged between culture(s), sciences, research and education; between specialised audience and broad public, between identities and nationalities.

The numerous intersections between the institutions, such as in the area of the libraries or in the Phonogramm-Archiv (Phonogram Archive) of the Ethnologisches Museum (Ethnological Museum) and the Lautarchiv (Sound Archive) of the Humboldt-Universität, not only allow an interlocking on a horizontal level, but also make possible vertical relationships throughout the entire building. Links in content and space with the exhibitions on the second and third floors will be generated by multifarious relationships in language, science, and ethnomusicology. Thus the canoes from the Oceanic exhibition of the Ethnologisches Museum, for example, are anchored in the cube on the first floor. The topic of communication will be explored in the Mesoamerica museum section on the second floor above the "World of Languages" of the Zentral- und Landesbibliothek. Not by chance can one discover here which similarities exist between the meaning of ancient indigenous sign languages and the icons of today's digital world.

Volker Heller

"World of Languages": The Zentral- und Landesbibliothek Berlin

Language, communication and intangible cultural heritage comprise the wealth of the world's cultures and form the basis for cultural dialogue, the principal theme of the activities at the Humboldt-Forum. The Zentral- und Landesbibliothek Berlin (ZLB, Central and Regional Library Berlin) has designed for the Humboldt-Forum a new type of space for educating and experiencing: the "World of Languages". It will present across 4,000 square metres on the first floor a place for language(s), other forms of expression, and transcultural communication. Here the ZLB aims to promote the diversity of languages and multilingualism, sensitising visitors to multiple communicative practices.

The "World of Languages" combines traditional library functions with innovative edutainment. Libraries see themselves largely as open, inviting places for education and learning. Edutainment, as a modern form of pedagogy, plays a key role in creating stimulating learning environments – especially in fields such as language learning and intercultural education. The "World of Languages" assumes a pioneering role by augmenting and modernising established library activities. With the support of scientific and educational partners the ZLB will offer in the "World of Languages" an attractive display window onto the cultural and linguistic variety of the city and its rich scientific and media landscape.

The edutainment area extends across some 1,200 square metres and will stimulate visitors to engage in self-directed experiences with linguistic phenomena and to explore the cognitive processes behind them. Similar to the formats of the science centre, which largely focuses on the natural sciences, the content will be presented in a visually attractive and intuitively comprehensible manner, by means of interactive games, short film clips, animations, and audio media. Visitors will learn playfully about the different aspects of language(s) and about the opportunities and obstacles of trans-cultural communication, linguistic variety and multilingualism. They will be made aware of and will learn to question the deceptions and prejudices to which our linguistic and cultural upbringing makes us all susceptible. Both spoken language and other forms of communication such as gestures, body language, dance and writing will be explored. The design of the "World of Languages" is currently under development and will feature state-of-the-art technologies when it is inaugurated. Current ideas could include a simulation demonstrating how a Mayan generally avoids direct eye contact, while in other cultures this is essential for conversation. Another simulation could present virtual interlocutors who prefer more or less physical distance according to their cultural background. A game could show how we evaluate such behaviour as either approachable, dismissive, or even intrusive.

The physical bridge between the edutainment and library areas will be formed by work rooms and booths equipped with permanently-installed multimedia and presentation equipment. The library area will have seating and reading places, a freely-accessible media stock, and offer a large amount of digital content. These media will be linked with the contents of the edutainment area and with the exhibitions and events at the Humboldt-Forum, but will also take up current discussions on the dialogue of cultures. One of the focuses of the "World of Languages" is on working with children and young people. Events will make this a lively place of learning, stimulating curiosity for other languages and cultures and encouraging and testing intercultural competence. The edutainment area, event programming and media stock will complement each other, so that visitors will experience the "World of Languages" as a thematic unity. The realisation of such an innovative space drives the ZLB into truly unexplored territory, even at the international level. Decisive challenges lie in the design and pedagogy of the media and in the orchestration of the individual applications into an integrated and appealing world of experience. The concept of the "World of Languages" is being currently worked out in a project sponsored by the European Union. The metropolis of Berlin is marked by the co-existence of and interchange among different cultures. This places a special responsibility on the city to make its position clear as well as supporting the dialogue of cultures both locally and globally. The "World of Languages" responds to this need. And no place could be more suitable for this than the Humboldt-Forum.

Facets of writing – The "A" Portal (detail) of the Berliner Stadtbibliothek (Berlin City Library) of the Zentral- und Landesbibliothek Berlin

Jan-Hendrik Olbertz

The Humboldt-Labor of the Humboldt-Universität zu Berlin

Within the Humboldt-Forum the Humboldt-Universität zu Berlin (Humboldt University of Berlin) will provide a platform for the field of science and make it comprehensible as a supporting pillar of our culture and of the everyday life of our society – for as broad a public as possible. The Humboldt-Universität zu Berlin, founded in 1810 and named after the Humboldt brothers in 1949, owes its pioneering idea of the unity of research and teaching to Wilhelm von Humboldt. Its guiding principle of "education through science" has been developed out of this idea and will inspire and direct the plans and concepts of the future Humboldt-Forum as well. The other Humboldt brother, Alexander, held his popular Cosmos lectures on the physical description of the world at the Berliner Universität; for us he represents a model and a challenge at the same time. Today scientists and students from over 130 countries work together at the Humboldt-Universität, networked with many research and teaching projects around the world. With their contacts and questions they will enliven as well as decisively shape the intercultural dialogue at the Humboldt-Forum.

At the Humboldt-Forum the Humboldt-Universität will present its own exhibition and event room, the Humboldt-Labor (Humboldt Laboratory), across an area of approximately 700 square metres. The public will be able to experience here key themes and current projects from university research and teaching, as well as from the history of science. Temporary exhibitions and events will demonstrate in a lively manner the role science plays in our everyday lives. The main focus will lie on introducing scientific procedures and methods of gaining knowledge, that is, making the methodological dimension of the creation of new knowledge transparent. Conversely, the Humboldt-Universität aims to demonstrate how everyday scientific life functions in the various scientific disciplines, whether in the laboratory, on research trips, or in archives. Closely linked to this is the presentation of the contemporary problems and issues of the future discussed by researchers around the world amongst themselves. They can range from life sciences and climate research to ethnological research and linguistic research. The Humboldt-Universität itself has great potential in this sphere, and in cooperation with scientific institutions, in particular with the neighbouring Zentral- und Landesbibliothek Berlin (Central and Regional Library Berlin) and its language focus, but also with the non-European collections of the Staatliche Museen zu Berlin (National Museums in Berlin), the variety of themes for exhibition projects at the Humboldt-Forum is almost inexhaustible. In all these ventures, however, the centre of attention will not be on a triumphal show of "finished" scientific results, but rather on methods and processes of cognition in scientific practice during the past and present – and that also includes controversies, speculations, errors, and limitations.

For these creative processes of design in the sciences the Humboldt-Universität will develop experimental forms of exhibition presentation, integrating objects from its wealth of historical and present-day teaching and research collections. Our exhibitions will not merely be presentations of the results of scientific work, but will transmit instead the process of research itself. In this manner they will allow, on the one hand, visitors to expand their knowledge, and on the other, they can become a creative component of scientists' dissemination and research activity. This dialogue between science and a broad public will not only take place in exhibitions, panels and talks. That is why performative events such as theatre pieces, science slams and school labs will be held, in which visitors of all ages and levels of previous knowledge and education can actively take part.

The Lautarchiv (Sound Archive) of the Humboldt-Universität, a valuable collection of sound documents from the first half of the twentieth century, will move into its own area. Over 7,500 gramophone records store spoken language and songs, among them original recordings of Rabindranath Tagore, Friedrich Ebert and Max Planck, as well as the systematic documentation of German dialects from 1922 on. Noteworthy in this archive are the sound documents in 250 different languages, recorded during World War I and the Weimar Republic. As the translation and precise information on the age, social background, and origins of the speakers have been preserved, these recordings are particularly valuable for linguistic research. With the joining of the Lautarchiv of the Humboldt-Universität and the Phonogramm-Archiv (Phonogram Archive) of the Staatliche Museen zu Berlin together under one roof in the Humboldt-Forum a unique collection of "voices of the world" will be created and made accessible to the public.

Improvement of decentralised water supply systems in Andhra Pradesh, India, a project in cooperative science at the Humboldt-Universität's Faculty of Agriculture and Horticulture, held in conjunction with the International Institute of Information Technology, Hyderabad, as part of "Sustainable Hyderabad", 2012

German-Cuban internships in plant molecular biology at the University of Havana in cooperation with the Humboldt-Universität zu Berlin, 2011

Lars-Christian Koch

The Media Collection of the Departments of Ethnomusicology, Media Technology and the Berlin Phonogramm-Archiv at the Ethnologisches Museum

For more than 100 years audio documents have transformed our perception of cultures as well as research on them; today they affect both aspects decisively. At the Humboldt-Forum this will be evident in many respects, with the historical depth of the media collection playing just as vital a role as its present-day collecting strategies. The scope of the Archive and Media Area of the Humboldt-Forum will be broad and dynamic, ranging from historical audio sound carriers to early photographs and films, up to and including today's global media pluralism. One of the main areas of focus in its planning and implementation will be its evolution into a cultural studies media centre.

The heart of the music archive – and an especially valuable part historically speaking – is the Berlin Phonogramm-Archiv (Phonogram Archive) housing approximately 16,000 original wax cylinder recordings. Such is its significance that it became the first German institution to be included in the UNESCO's Memory of the World list in 1999. In many respects it is one of the most important and comprehensive collections of historical musical cultures in the world. Founded in 1900 by Professor Carl Stumpf of the Psychologisches Institut der Berliner Universität (Psychological Institute at the Berlin University), its interest was initially focused on aspects relating to acoustics and music psychology, while Stumpf's successor Erich Moritz von Hornbostel soon established close ties and successful collaboration with the former Museum für Völkerkunde (Museum of Ethnology) in Berlin. The principle objective was now to collect as many examples as possible of the most diverse musical cultures, in order to formulate and to expand theories on the origins and

page 73
Edison Heim Phonograph and a
selection of wax cylinders, ca. 1905

evolution of music. Based on the great number of wax cylinder recordings from all over the world a new academic discipline was thus first created in Berlin: comparative musicology, today known as ethnomusicology.

The wax cylinders collected between 1893 and 1954 from almost all regions of the world have been catalogued together with the correspondence, literary excerpts and photographs. After World War II the purchase of a tape recorder initiated a new era of recording technology. A sound archive was created that continues to focus on field research recordings and at present comprises almost 13,000 hours of magnetic tape material in a variety of data formats. This archive is complemented by a continuously growing stock of audio-visual recordings and commercial sound carriers from recent research for two reasons: firstly, to supply reference material for research purposes and, secondly, to open up further possibilities for the area of media studies with basic data that is as comprehensive as possible.

The department's present-day work will be disseminated at the Humboldt-Forum primarily through the documentation of research activities and current research projects. Here it will be crucial to demonstrate that ethnomusicology goes beyond a purely historical framework and has evolved into field of cultural study with numerous interdisciplinary links. Ethnomusicology also incorporates urban music research, which naturally must integrate the scientific, performative and pedagogical study of Berlin's musical cultures.

Box with phonogram cylinders
from Africa, ca. 1905

The first floor of the Humboldt-Forum will also house the Lautarchiv (Sound Archive) of the Humboldt-Universität zu Berlin (Humboldt University of Berlin), which was located until 1934 together with the Phonogramm-Archiv at the Berliner Universität and was similarly based on the work of the Prussian Phonogram Commission under its chairman Carl Stumpf. At the Humboldt-Forum both collections will once again be made available and presented in one place. A project funded by the Deutsche Forschungs-gemeinschaft (German Research Council) for the cataloguing and digitalisation of both of the collections, with emphasis on the Phonogramm-Archiv, was begun in 2013 and will be completed in 2016.

The media department will have an extensive range of offerings for dissemination available. The mezzanine between the first and second floors will house the Sound Work-shop of the Department of Ethnomusicology, Media Technology and Berlin Phono-gramm-Archiv in a multifunctional room, in which instruments will be permanently dis-played. They will include the large gamelan orchestra from the collection of the Ethnologisches Museum, but also specially-built or created instruments for pedagogical purposes. At the same time, this area can be quickly adapted for concerts, performances, lectures and small conferences of up to 100 people, as well as for workshops, such as on musical practice, instrument making, music production, or media design. Here is where the existing diverse activities in the field of pedagogical projects and concert events will be continued and expanded. A glassed-in studio adjacent to the sound workshop will make the work of the Department of Ethnomusicology, Media Technology, and Berlin Phono-gramm-Archiv comprehensible to the broad public, but also provide external possibilities of use for universities, schools and adult education. At the same time, it will technically assist and document performances and pedagogical events. Audio-visual stations in the library areas will allow visitors to the Humboldt-Forum to become acquainted with the sounds of the most varied cultures. The stations will also offer visitors the possibility of thoroughly engaging with sound and music languages, as well as the performance details inherent to them, under visual aspects. In this manner perspectives of acoustic phenomena in the sense of forms of human communication will be explored and disseminated.

Ethnomusicology is a trans-regional science that has its roots in Berlin. Since musical practices in today's global environment can no longer be regionally situated, a differen-tiated representation of this insight will be necessary in contemporary media as well. This is to be achieved through accompanying ethnomusicological themes in the regional areas of the exhibitions in the Humboldt-Forum.

Moritz Wullen/Richard Haas/Uta Rahman-Steinert

The Library of Non-European Art and Cultures

Together with the Ethnologisches Museum (Ethnological Museum) and the Museum für Asiatische Kunst (Asian Art Museum), the Kunstbibliothek (Art Library) is planning a research library for non-European art and cultures for the Humboldt-Forum. This library will unite the holdings of the Ethnologisches Museum and the Museum für Asiatische Kunst that have evolved over time to unite a wide variety of disciplines: ethnology, ethnomusicology, East Asian and Indian art and cultural history, American archaeology, ethnohistory and religious studies. A further focus will lie on the literature of exploration and travel as well as on publications from colonial and missionary history. For the new installation of this library its approximately 150,000 volumes will be catalogued according to international standards and to a great extent placed in open stacks. Research on the collection, library use and electronic information will be efficiently integrated in a joint working area. The public library is planned as a reference library. It will have a gallery in the reading area, a working room for groups and several small studios for audio-visual media. Offices for guest scholars will be available as well.

Literature relating to the investigation of the world's cultures was already collected by the Königliche Museen (Royal Museums) before the foundation of an independent ethnological museum in 1873. These holdings constituted the basis for the library of the former Museum für Völkerkunde (Museum for Ethnology) when it received its own building on Stresemannstrasse in 1886. Of great importance was the contractual agreement which had the Berliner Gesellschaft für Anthropologie, Ethnologie und Urgeschichte (Berlin Society for Anthropology, Ethnology, and Prehistory) set up its library in the museum's rooms. Despite the removal of parts of the holdings of books and journals during World War II, there were substantial losses due to fire, water damage and plundering. After the gradual expansion of the holdings, the library of the Ethnologisches Museum today alone consists of over 107,000 volumes and about 300 current periodicals. It is regarded as the largest and most important ethnological library in the German-speaking region.

Umbständliche und Eigentliche

Beschreibung

von

AFRICA,

Und denen darzu gehörigen Königreichen und Landschaften/

als

Egypten/ Barbarien/ Libyen/ Biledulgerid/ dem Lande der Negros/ Guinea/ Ethiopien/ Abyßina/ und den Africanischen Insulen:

Zusamt deren

Verscheidenen Nahmen/ Grentzen/ Städten/ Flüssen/ Gewächsen/ Thieren/ Sitten/ Trachten / Sprachen/ Reichthum/ Gottesdienst / und Regierung.

Wobey

Die Land-Carten/ und Abrisse der Städte/ Trachten/ ꝛc. in Kupfer.

Auß unterschiedlichen neuen Land- und Reise-Beschreibungen mit fleiß zusammen gebracht

Durch

O. DAPPER, Dr.

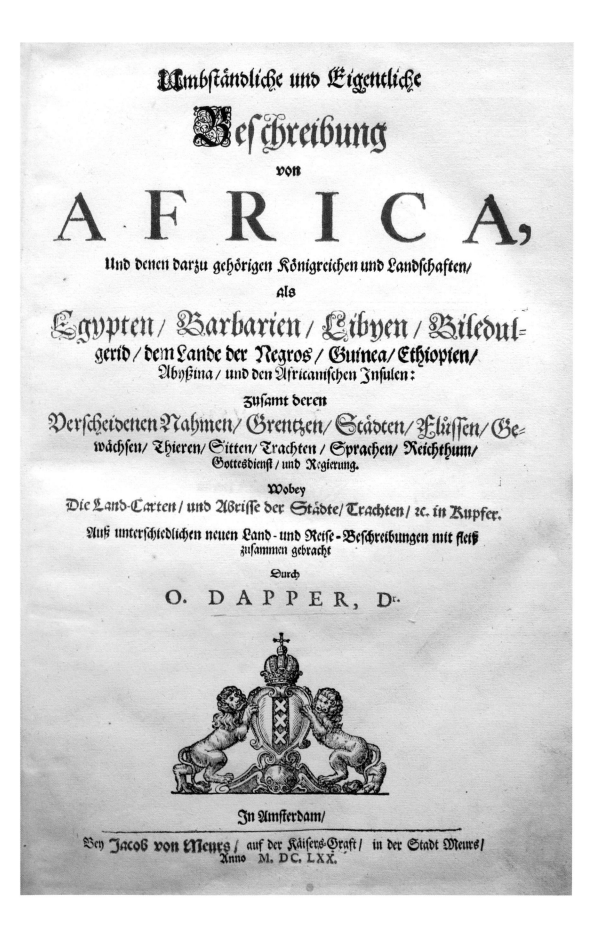

In Amsterdam/

Bey Jacob von Meurs/ auf der Käisers-Graft/ in der Stadt Meurs/ Anno M. DC. LXX.

page 77
O. Dapper, *Umbständliche und Eigentliche Beschreibung von Africa, Und denen darzu gehörigen Königreichen und Landschaften …*, [Extensive and Actual Description of Africa and its Kingdoms and Landscapes…], Amsterdam 1670, title page

The library of the Museum für Asiatische Kunst consists of two independent sub-libraries, formed when the former museums for East Asian and Indian Art were merged. The extensive specialised library of the Ostasiatische Kunstsammlung (East Asian Art Collection) was famous in its time and built up in parallel to the museum founded in 1906. The entire library, however, was destroyed by fire during a bomb attack on 3 February 1945. Founded again after the war, it unites in approximately 20,000 volumes and 100 current periodicals literature on East Asian art history, archaeology and the decorative arts of East Asia from the Neolithic period to the present day, almost half of the holdings being from China, Japan, and Korea. The library of the art collection of South, Southeast, and Central Asia collects literature on the art, archaeology, religious and cultural history of the Indian subcontinent and Southeast and Central Asia, from the Harappan period to the present. With its approximately 15,000 volumes and 60 current periodicals it represents the only specialised library of its kind in Germany. Because of the major extension of their subject areas, both libraries concentrate on building up holdings related to their art collections, most recently including literature on contemporary art in the relevant regions.

With the installation of the libraries of the Ethnologisches Museum and the Museum für Asiatische Kunst at the Humboldt-Forum and with the inauguration of this library over more than 1,800 square metres, the Kunstbibliothek – which will have overall responsibility for the new library – will become one of the world's largest museum libraries with a service network of three locations: Kulturforum Potsdamer Platz (art library and museum collections), Archäologisches Zentrum (archaeological library), and Humboldt-Forum (library of non-European art and cultures). As in its other branches, at the Humboldt-Forum the Kunstbibliothek aims to provide as comprehensive and as differentiated a range of literature as possible, geared to the focuses of the museums' collections. Purchases are made from the library's own funds and with the support of the Deutsche Forschungsgemeinschaft (DFG, German Research Council). One of the areas of focus of the current DFG financing is the acquisition of books on international contemporary art from the non-European cultures in the regions of Africa, South Asia, East Asia, and Oceania.

The new branch of the Kunstbibliothek will likewise not be open solely for curators of the collections and guest scholars. It will also address students, university lecturers and all those interested in art and culture who want to make an intensive study of the objects in the non-European collections. A special concern is the unlimited access to publications from non-European linguistic and cultural areas. With a view towards the future location at the Humboldt-Forum, the Kunstbibliothek is working at high speed on the digital retroconversion of its card catalogues and, with the financial support of the DFG, the new cataloguing of titles in non-European languages. The objective hereby is to augment on a lasting basis the attraction of the holdings for external scholars.

With the new library at the Humboldt-Forum the museums are reacting to the growing globalisation of their research. The view of the collections' objects in a context within the history of civilisations has made way for a new perspective. The history of art and culture is now regarded as a network, one in which the most different of histories

IV

Rabitans des îles Aléoutiennes.

co-exist and interact with one another. Thanks to the communication possibilities of the Internet, the growing mobility of scientists, international research and digitalisation projects, and fellowship and exchange programmes, the sciences too are rapidly being internationalised and scientific fields of growth are increasingly networked with one another. Researchers from all over the world are together discovering a fascinating variety of regional and trans-regional art and cultural histories.

In the light of such a "global turn", the planned library of non-European art and cultures represents a trendsetting pilot project. Its acquisition and service profile is being defined by the library scientists of the Kunstbibliothek, the museum curators of the Ethnologisches Museum and the Museum für Asiatische Kunst, and by representatives from Berlin's universities and other important libraries. Special focus is placed on the "net generation" (those born in 1990 and after), who during the course of this decade will be supplying the junior academic staff. They utilise with great success the information supplied in search machines, blogs, virtual work environments and online encyclopaedias, in order to build up their individual libraries on global art literature. Their experiences, desires and expectations are to influence the conception of the library. The ultimate objective is an information and literature centre for the history of non-European art and culture, one which can react flexibly and find creative answers to the changing demands made on the provision of scholarly information in the far future as well.

Louis Choris, *Voyage pittoresque autour du monde, avec des portraits de sauvages d'Amérique, d'Asie, d'Afrique, et des îles du Grand Océan …* [Picturesque Voyage Around the World, with Portraits of the Savages of America, Asia, Africa, and of the Islands of the Great Ocean…], Paris 1822, fol. IV

Setting Sail:
A New Departure
for our Museums

The two upper floors of the Humboldt-Forum will be reserved for reconfigurations of the Ethnologisches Museum (Ethnological Museum) and the Museum für Asiatische Kunst (Asian Art Museum). Expectations are high and the opportunities gained by locating these two major collections in the rebuilt Berliner Schloss (Berlin Palace) pose a great challenge. Both museums are currently developing cross-cultural and cross-institutional concepts for this reorganisation with regard to realising content as well as topical issues. In addition to their historically evolved collections, a greater emphasis than before is to be placed on aspects of contemporary art, new forms of expression and the relationships between artists and their environment. Connections and contexts come to the fore; key themes such as the "the present," "multiperspectivity" and "the audience" define new priorities and strategies for collecting, research, communication and presentation.

The museums are involved in productive discussions with the planners and designers of Ralph Appelbaum Associates/malsyteufel about the exhibition design together with the use of new media and technologies. In addition to the established formats of film, video, audio and the internet, these include modern "virtual companions" as well as electronic labelling and guidance systems and, last not least, furnishing stage areas, performance spaces and lecture halls both inside and outside of the museums with media equipment.

The concepts presented here reflect the current status as well as the planning horizon. Within the next two years these content-related concepts will be finalised and realised in collaboration with the design team along with the actual selection of exhibits, which include numerous items of great value and major importance.

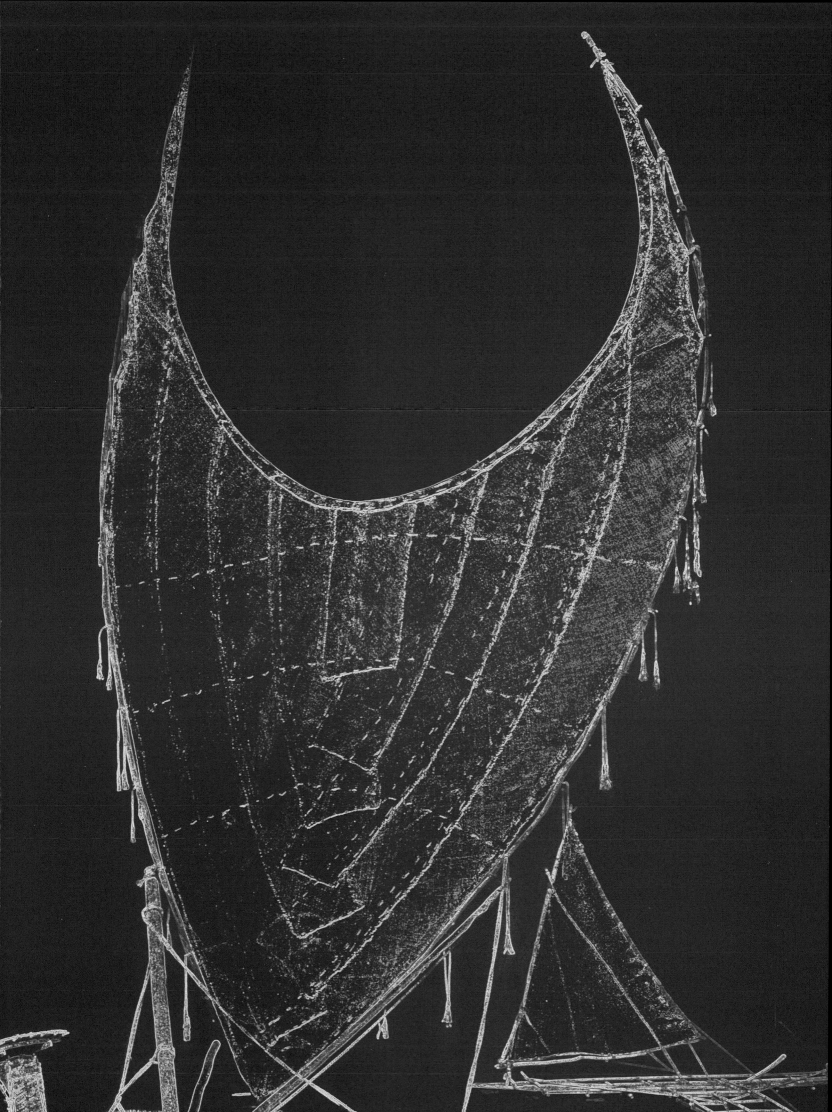

Viola König

Worlds in Motion: The Ethnologisches Museum at the Humboldt-Forum

Introduction

Expectations on the contents of the Humboldt-Forum are high. The reconstructed Berliner Schloss (Berlin Palace) should not simply house a single museum made up of two of the Staatliche Museen zu Berlin (National Museums in Berlin). In conjunction with events and special exhibitions on the ground floor areas, library holdings from the Zentral- und Landesbibiliothek Berlin (Central and Regional Library Berlin) as well as from the museums themselves and from the Humboldt-Labor (Humboldt Laboratory) of Humboldt-Universität zu Berlin (Humboldt University of Berlin), the collections of the museums at the Berliner Schloss will enter into an open-minded dialogue with the cultures of the world, thus establishing a forum that is truly novel: the Humboldt-Forum. For the museums this is a challenge that requires them to engage in a delicate balancing act between their traditional self-understanding as an institution committed to collecting, preserving and exhibiting and forum based on exhibits and new media which aims at a blend of dialogue and entertainment. At the Humboldt Lab Dahlem these expectations are tested in practice: the objects present themselves in unusual contexts and convey new and multiple messages. Artists operate not just as creators of artworks, but also as curators of content; media are deployed as agents on equal terms with the exhibits. Old constraints and entrenched thought structures of museum specialists and conservators are questioned. These experiments are intended to provoke, but must be checked at the same time for their compatibility with the development of the master plan for the exhibition spaces.

In the twenty-first century all ethnological museums, indeed, face issues and challenges that profoundly affect their self-understanding and approach to their collections: what to present in what manner to which visitors? Should ethnographic museums emphasise their close links with the colonial legacy, as has been demanded in the post-colonial debate, or rather focus on contemporary relevance in their collecting policies and exhibitions? Who is entitled to possess and display the material remains of "other" cultures? Can new models of curatorial practice and/or demands raised by contemporary ethnological

page 83
Arrangement of the sailboats
from the Santa Cruz Islands, 1960,
at the Ethnologisches Museum,
Berlin-Dahlem, 2012

theory break up old power structures and re-adjust the – European-induced – imbalance from earlier periods?

These are by no means just academic dry runs, but rather central ideas when visualising the expected clientèle at the Humboldt-Forum as both national and international visitors with widely varied interests: citizens of Berlin, including a growing number of members of international communities from all continents; tourists from all over the world, increasingly also from the countries of origin of the displayed objects; and, last but not least, specialists and artists participating in programmes of the Humboldt-Forum. In short, visitors will be highly diverse and their expectations regarding the Humboldt-Forum will not necessarily be compatible.

The way it sees itself, the Humboldt-Forum is not an institution focusing on a single theme, a single issue. It concerns itself with culture and history (or histories) from all continents, but its approach starts inevitably from a European perspective. The concept of multi-perspective presentation and shifts in narrative point of view are intended to ensure not just a single perspective, but rather varying views of subjects and exhibits. What does this mean specifically for the Ethnologisches Museum (Ethnological Museum) at the Humboldt-Forum?

1. For the first time in its history, the Ethnologisches Museum will present itself as a unified whole with coherent concepts regarding its regional collection segments. In 1881, the museum's original building at Stresemannstrasse was erected without such concepts

Sketch of the new Boat Hall arrangement including a visible storage, Ralph Appelbaum Associates/malsy-teufel, 2013

and even in Dahlem post-war history led to additive exhibitions that, from 1956 on, opened in different decades. For the first time, the Ethnologisches Museum and the Museum für Asiatische Kunst (Asian Art Museum) are now being planned jointly and old reservations are being overcome.

2. The focus areas of the collections are presented and commented on from different and sometimes provocative perspectives. These shifts in focus zero in on artistic expressions and historical developments as well as on the classic ethnological questions, wherever possible in consultation with representatives of the cultures presented. This by itself implies a shift in narrative viewpoints. Authorship is no longer assumed just by the museum's permanent staff, but by other actors and narrators as well.

3. The collections will be scrutinised in chronological depth, both with regard to the understanding of their own and extrinsic roots and as possible keys to an awareness of current global developments and processes. The modes of communicating socio-political debates are subject to shifting questions, expectations and media-related developments. The challenge in realising the Humboldt-Forum is to do justice to these aspirations of a "museum in motion."

The multiple human being: vision, statements and messages

In the nineteenth century, the vision of the Ethnologisches Museum's founding father, Adolf Bastian, focused on saving the material remains of "vanishing cultures". Likewise his famous student, Franz Boas, the father of American cultural anthropology, aspired to record and archive entire cultures. With this in mind, German collectors in particular amassed

Model of the new Boat Hall arrangement, Ralph Appelbaum Associates/ malsyteufel, 2013

Design of the Mesoamerica exhibition segment with Lienzo Seler II, Ralph Appelbaum Associates/ malsyteufel, 2013

extensive bodies of artefacts from America, Africa, Asia and Oceania for the Museum für Völkerkunde (Museum of Ethnology) in Berlin. As a result, the present-day Ethnologisches Museum possesses over half a million objects, complemented by 140,000 audio records, 285,000 historical photographs and 50,000 metres of film footage. Arising from this wealth of material are not just presentation options for the curators, but also duties with regard to the objects concerned. The Ethnologisches Museum is in a unique position to illustrate cultural diversity, the ways of human existence in dealing with the environment and man as a social being and as an artist, as well as many other topics on the basis of specific examples. It can challenge visitors and confront them with issues. It is traditionally

strong in addressing, in special ways, children, young people and families; it arouses and satisfies curiosity and contributes to the cultural education of open-minded, tolerant citizens of the world. This endeavour is, indeed, reflective of both the spirit of the Humboldt-Forum and the typical mission of an ethnological museum in the twenty-first century.

Of a museum with such heterogeneous, cultural-historical and global aspirations one also expects topical debates that go beyond appealing displays. Are there cross-cultural topics that are as important to us today as to our ancestors or to the members of "foreign" cultures and periods? What is still relevant today, what is not, or no longer, and why? The exhibitions of the Ethnologisches Museum at the Humboldt-Forum always touch on "grand themes" as well – *Der mobile Mensch* (Mobile Man), for example, on the issues of people in motion, migration and trade; *Der gläubige Mensch* (Religious Man) on belief systems, world views and ideologies; *Der Mensch und seine Umwelt* (Man and His Environment) on environmental practices and cognition; *Der Mensch als Erfinder und Nachahmer* (Man as an Inventor and Imitator) on genius, cultural transfer, devising and copying; *Der Mensch als Ästhet* (Man as an Aesthete) on artisans' and artists' expressions; *Mensch und Macht* (Man and Power) on leadership, system preservation and conflicts; *Der Mensch und sein Lebensweg* (Man and His Life's Journey) on the complexes of rites of passage and rituals; and *Mensch und Körper* (Man and Body) on health and disease, medicine and body images.

Within the framework of these general topics and with aesthetically appealing presentations, the museums at the Humboldt-Forum will present themselves as both a cultural-historical archive and a global network – open to a topical scholarly, artistic and media-based discourse.

Multiperspectivity, diversity of voices and perspective shifts

Multiperspectivity means basic thematic positioning: within a dynamic conception and choice of subjects and objects, various actors emerge. Multiperspectivity implies an awareness and consideration of the fact that objects are viewed in ways that are subject to historical shifts and a continuous process of (re-)appropriation and (re-)interpretation. Multiperspectivity at the Humboldt-Forum therefore involves both a synchronous and a diachronous approach, resulting in "a plurality of truth." In its consistent further development, this approach leads to a diversity of voices, as there is a demand not just for the perspectives of external consultants, but for their curatorial input as well. They will have their "say" at the Humboldt-Forum. Old classification systems and prerogatives of interpretation are scrutinised. For example, ethnologists in the past liked to take the alleged position of the authors or descendants of the donor culture, while art historians tended to consider the artworks in isolation. Such contradictory positions are being dismantled today and the voices of present-day descendants of the donor cultures play an increasingly important role. The concept for the Ethnologisches Museum at the Humboldt-Forum allows for all those approaches and views them not as conflicting, but rather as a potential.

The narrative presentation from various viewpoints also traces the movement of objects through space and time around the globe, with constantly changing interpretations being reflected even in conservatorial treatment. For instance, where necessary, the presentation at the Humboldt-Forum will have to take into account directives and taboos linked to clearly identified objects, while extreme conservatorial approaches that are sometimes completely at odds with destruction practices in the countries of origin need to be relaxed.

The interpretative dominance of European museum experts has been questioned by 1990s post-colonial critique – down to the point of view that only members of the particular culture are able to decipher and assess "their" objects. Yet they do not take into account the re-appropriation of cultural techniques and contents as part of the twentieth-century cultural revival strategies of indigenous groups, which are based specifically on the

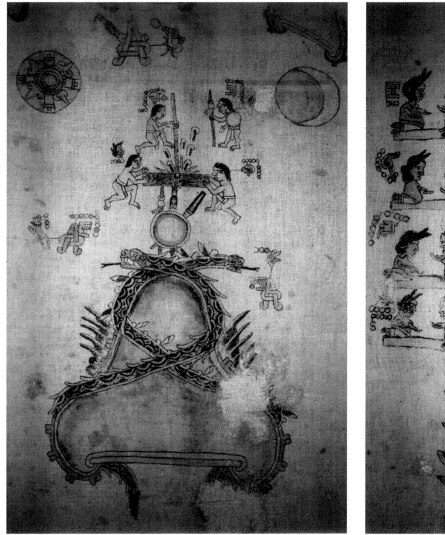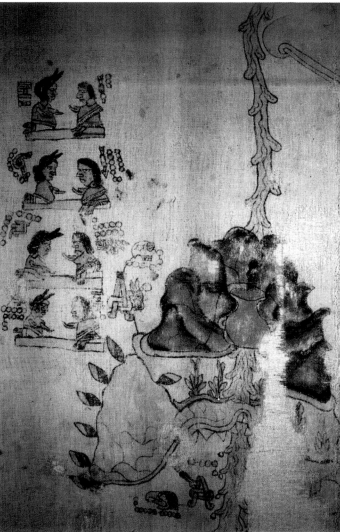

scholarly works of Western experts and documents of European collectors. Re-interpretations lead to new meanings. Others, by contrast, tend to go mostly unnoticed: most of the collections in European museums were created from a male perspective; women were a minority among collectors. Hence museums are veritable weapons stockpiles, whereas the world of women was usually inaccessible to male Europeans. Present-day indigenous representatives are quite pragmatic and, occasionally, positive about the preservation of objects in a European museum, provided they are guaranteed access to them. Visible storages at the Humboldt-Forum offer access without curatorial interference. Irrespective of this, the goal of multiperspectivity and multidisciplinarity is vividness. Involving artists in a dialogue with researchers may serve to create new experiences, to be able to convey those experiences to visitors and promote the comfort factor in exhibition practice.

Lienzo Seler II, Mexico, Oaxaca, before 1556 (details)

"Non-Europe"? – colonialism and global history

The political division of the world into "The West and the Rest" is rooted in the colonial era, which resulted in the construction of a non-European world: over here a developed

Europe that was politically, culturally and economically superior, and over there the backward, foundering world of the unsuccessful who had no choice but to bow to the political and economic interests of Europe. Ethnographic collections, which developed analogously, carry this politically and ideologically motivated division forward to this day. Since colonial times their province has been the separate history and culture of the non-European world. In 1884-85, the Berlin-Congo Conference, at which the European powers negotiated the colonial division of Africa, was held not far from the Humboldt-Forum, in the Reichskanzlei (Reich Chancellery) at Wilhelmstrasse 77. At the Humboldt-Forum there is a need to address the fragmentation of the world, a need to open up new perspectives on history and the present, in order to provide – as a forum in the true sense of the word – the setting for a discursive process.

The Berlin collections in the heart of Berlin – both at Museum Island and at the Deutsches Historisches Museum (German Historical Museum) – are the result of historical processes that are directly related to the emergence of trade capitalism in Europe, the development of shipping and the concomitant opening up of the world for Europe. It is impossible to understand – or to tell – the history of the individual continents without taking into account this process. At the Humboldt-Forum the separation between Europe and "non-Europe" is lifted. Rather than being directed from Berlin at exotic foreign worlds, the perspective of the exhibitions incorporates Europe. The challenge is to overcome one-sided post-colonial perceptions that place the European museums squarely in the tradition of colonialism and construe the non-European world as a victim of colonialism, thereby perpetuating the fragmentation of the world.

There is invariably a socio-political dimension to multiperspectivity. Berlin is home to people with an "immigrant background" which, in the vast majority of cases, does not correspond to the overseas cultures addressed by the museums at the Humboldt-Forum. This is yet another reason why a multiperspectival approach ensures the perception and discussion of social and cultural change – of "motion" in the world, in our climes and especially in Berlin.

Modernity and contemporary art

Forms of expression of twentieth- and twenty-first-century art from Asia, Latin and North America, Africa, Australia and the South Pacific are an important component of the Humboldt-Forum, not just in the spaces for special exhibitions on the ground floor, but also in the exhibition areas of the two museums on the second and third floors. Many contemporary artists from overseas still demur at being exhibited in an ethnological museum and thereby becoming "ethnicised." However, at the Humboldt-Forum in the centre of Berlin this may change. Ideally, the art exhibited at the Humboldt-Forum both addresses current global developments and reflects on the pre-European and colonial periods. The Humboldt-Forum lends itself as a venue for artists in residence or for artist's talks, while the visible storages in the exhibition spaces are a great resource for studying the material art and culture. Allegedly historical objects and historical artworks play a role in the present and can be queried for issues that are relevant today. This requires an acquisition policy on the part of the museums that is open to contem-

Throne, Cameroon, Bamun, 19th century

Patchwork coat of a Dervish, Iran, mid-19th century

porary art and that naturally incorporates "immaterial culture," be it film, video, audio or the internet.

A Junior Museum in the heart of Berlin

Young visitors, schoolchildren and young people, in a group, with the family or alone, should feel at ease at the Humboldt-Forum and sense that they are particularly welcome as one of the major target groups. At the Humboldt-Forum, the sites focused on their particular interests will not be found at marginal locations, separate from the main exhibition area, but are interspersed throughout the area as exhibition and activity spaces of equal status. Adjacent exhibition themes and object groups are playfully incorporated and subjected to media-based treatment. Though clearly delimited, their particular configuration renders these discovery centres and activity labs permeable to the main exhibitions.

Neck pendant, Brazil, Urubu-Ka'apor,
20th century

The basic structure: exhibition modules, meeting points and visible storages

Clear guidance within the dramatic composition of an exhibition space of over 16,000 square metres is a pre-requisite for visitors to feel at ease, to stay for an extended period of time and to want to return, again and again, to the Humboldt-Forum. The basic geographic breakdown by continents traditionally applied at ethnological museums has proved itself, since it satisfies the first query of a typical visitor of this type of museum regarding the "where." However, transcontinental transitions will demonstrate that cultures do not conform to an artificial division of the world into continents. Deliberate disruptions and overarching "grand themes" not tied to a particular region provide the concept's framework. In addition to the junior museums mentioned above, each of the four "continent areas" will include meeting points, visible storages and thematic modules.

Discovery Centre at the Te Papa National Museum, New Zealand, Wellington

Meeting points: Large objects which have been integrated into the master plan for the museum's collection will be used to help create an atmospheric layout of such ensembles of spaces. These objects will range from house models and boats from Oceania and totem poles from the Northwest coast of North America to stelae from Cotzumalhuapa in Mesoamerica and a tea house in the spaces of the Museum für Asiatische Kunst. Such meeting points allow various kinds of uses: seating accommodations invite visitors to relax and examine the topics that interest them in greater depth through the media; and at the same time these areas can be used as spaces for smaller events, concerts or performances.

Visible storages: each of the four "continent areas" will incorporate a visible storage as an independent module offering curious visitors access to previously hidden holdings, which they can explore at their own discretion or by means of media stations. They also provide specialists such as expert scholars, students, artists and designers with a wealth of illustrative material beyond the edited exhibitions. The organisation of the visible storages and the selection of exhibits will be based on varying criteria and topics and may, for instance, take the form of entire collections packed into a few square metres: jewellery, paintings, shadow puppets or textiles in pull-out drawers or hanging file folders, accompanied by digital documentation. Important topics include the history of the collections and collecting strategies, including problematic modes of appropriation during the colonial era. When not on display within the exhibition modules, major highlights from the holdings of the museums will thus be ever-present at the Humboldt-Forum; a continuous exchange with the stocks will be made possible.

Thematic modules: subjects and narratives of the exhibition modules will alternate, while avoiding content overlap. Sufficient space is devoted to each topic in order to present the focal areas of the collections appropriately and to steer clear of detailed, encyclopaedic accounts of the kind one would traditionally find in ethnographic museums. Modules and topics will change every eight years at the latest to ensure that all core collections of the Ethnologisches Museum and all possible topics will continue to be presented in an up-to-date manner.

Tours of the museum

Alternative points of access direct visitors to the exhibits. The Oceania section on the second floor leads to the Boat Hall and the clubhouses on the first floor. Through the music ethnology section one reaches Africa where one can leave the exhibits or, alternatively, move on to America. The Africa and America exhibits can each be accessed directly as well. The third floor is devoted to Asia and includes exhibits by the Ethnologisches Museum and the Museum für Asiatische Kunst, which can be explored by way of a tour of the entire floor or in individual stages.

Oceania and Australia: To date, painting from Oceania has received scant attention in museums, which tend to focus instead on the carvings. It is intended that this will change at the Humboldt-Forum. Paintings on bark cloths, palm leaf sheaths and shields offer a unique survey of styles and painting techniques used in Oceania. Among the exhibits are gable walls of Maprik houses, large palm leaf paintings from New Guinea, bark paintings from Australia and tapa from Polynesia. "Palau and Colonial Encounters" is the topic of the meeting point: a Palau house and beam as well as the House of the Spirits, displayed for the first time at the Humboldt-Forum, will be presented with Abelam houses and a newly acquired initiation chamber. The large boats and a faithful reproduction that may be accessed can be admired within the thematic module titled "Ships, Environment, Cognitive Systems and Navigation." The topics of this module include cognitive systems, adaptation to the environment, intensive use of resources and settlement history. Quintessentially associated with motion, the boats are an important identifying feature for many Pacific Islanders.

Africa: The focus is on an exemplary account of the history of Africa that does not ignore connections and context. African societies were – and are – actors in common historical processes that link this continent to Asia, America and Europe. The "Indian Ocean" module presents pre-European contacts with Asia and, later on, with Europe, the "History of the Benin Empire" module the interwovenness through triangular trade with

Meeting point Palau Islands
clubhouse, 1900

Europe, Africa and America. Africa's contact with Europe during the German colonial period is addressed within the module "Art and History of the Cameroon Grasslands." Contemporary representatives of, say, the Benin Empire and the kingdoms of the Cameroon grasslands will present their own views of history within the exhibition. "Contemporary Art/Present" reflects on Africa's current relations to America and Europe, for instance by using the example of African communities in Berlin.

Nontsikelelo Veleko, Beauty is in the Eye of the Beholder: Nonkululeko, 2003

America: In the New World prior to the arrival of the Europeans, sophisticated writing and calendar systems existed only in Mesoamerica. In addition to the "complete" writing system of the Maya, non-linguistic communication systems based on pictographs were developed, with obvious connections to present-day simultaneous text- and image-based communication. The 18-square-metre cotton cloth of the Lienzo Seler II offers connections to the present with genealogies of local rulers, accounts of war-like conflicts, Spanish evangelisation as well as cartographical elements; media-facilitated interconnectedness with the original region in Oaxaca and current archaeological digs help transform this dead piece of cloth into a living landscape. In the immediately adjacent pre-Columbian golden chamber the search for "El Dorado" is explained by Alexander von Humboldt himself. An assembly space from the Pacific Northwest is directly linked, as a meeting point, to the totem poles and the thematic module called "One Collection – Two Perspectives – The Voyage of Captain Jacobsen to the Northwest coast and Alaska." Here indigenous history and European expansion are considered from various viewpoints. The second floor tour ends with the transcontinental thematic module "The Circum-Pacific Modernism."

Asia: On the third floor, the Ethnologisches Museum and the Museum für Asiatische Kunst are showcasing focal areas of their collections, with a particular emphasis on representing the religions of Islam, Daoism, Confucianism, Buddhism and folk religions. One of the thematic modules is devoted to the encounter of the Orient and Occident. The collection focusing on Qajar Persia (1779–1925), with additional examples from the Ottoman Empire and historic photographs, illustrates the political opening and rapprochement of Iran and the Ottoman Empire toward the West. The meeting point presents "The World of Asian Theatre," with performances in front of the screen, on the stage, and with original musical instruments. Shadow, mask and puppet theatre from Indonesia, Thailand, Myanmar, India and China comes alive with various rod puppets, masks and marionettes. The tour of the Asia floor ends with an installation that immerses visitors in an abundance of colourful textiles from all over the world.

Conclusion

The above outline reflects content-related plans as of 2013. It is based on the detailed concept of the Ethnologisches Museum from 2008 (see Viola König and Andrea Scholz, in *Humboldt-Forum: Der lange Weg 1999–2012* [Berlin, 2012]), which has been continuously updated over the past five years by the editors Peter Junge, Markus Schindlbeck, Andrea Scholz and Monika Zessnik, as well as by the curators of the Ethnologisches Museum. The master plan for the design of the Humboldt-Forum presented by Ralph Appelbaum Associates/malsyteufel in November of 2012 now necessitates commitments regarding the inaugural installation that can only marginally be further modified. The major challenge for the coming years of the construction phase will be to integrate new impulses, ideas and insights generated particularly by the Humboldt Lab Dahlem and by current academic debates into the conception.

Mixtec municipal representatives of Santa Maria Cuquila in Oaxaca, Mexico, studying the facsimile edition of a pre-Hispanic codex thought to originate from their community, 2008

Klaas Ruitenbeek

The Museum für Asiatische Kunst at the Humboldt-Forum: New Tasks in a Globalized World

Nearly the entire fourth floor of the Humboldt-Forum is dedicated to Asia. Here the Museum für Asiatische Kunst (Asian Art Museum) and the Ethnologisches Museum (Ethnological Museum) present the art, culture and ethnology of that continent, with all their riches, from the earliest periods to the present, from art for the élite to popular culture and daily life, thereby enabling visitors to experience them. The Museum für Asiatische Kunst was founded by Wilhelm von Bode in 1906 as an art museum; in more than a century since then it has continuously expanded its collections with works of art acquired primarily for aesthetic reasons and has shown them to the public in numerous exhibitions.

At its current location in Berlin-Dahlem, the Museum für Asiatische Kunst is divided into two large sections, which until 2006 were separate museums, each with its own history: the Department of East Asian Art and the Department of South, Southeast and Central Asian art. The museum's collection includes around 34,000 objects, from all parts of Asia east of Iran, making it one of the largest and most important museums of such art in Europe. Whereas the collections from Southeast Asia, Korea and the Himalaya region are comparatively small, the museum is distinguished by its comprehensive collections of all genres of art from South Asia. They include outstanding Indian sculptures, in which the art of the Gandhara Region is particularly well represented. The Islamic era and the colonial period are present in high-quality examples of Indian crafts as well as by important holdings of Indian painting and historical photographs. The Central Asian collection, which was collected along the northern Silk Road in Xinjiang, China, between 1902 and 1914, is also spectacular, despite considerable losses during wartime, with considerable numbers of impressive works of high artistic quality. The museum also has extensive, high-quality

page 99

The Cave of the Ring-Bearing Doves, China, Kizil, 5th or 6th century. Reconstruction with original murals in the Museum für Asiatische Kunst, Berlin-Dahlem, 2012

holdings of painting, graphic arts, ceramics and the applied arts from East Asia from the period after the year 1000. Early bronzes and ceramics from China are also represented by exquisite examples. Roughly two thousand of the museum's works are currently exhibited to the public: 1,200 in the exhibition spaces and 800 in an accessible study collection. The other objects are kept in closed study collections that are used by scholars from all over the world.

The exhibition in Dahlem aims to provide visitors with an overall aesthetic experience while also presenting each object as an individual work of art. The arrangement is based primarily on cultural regions and genres and is largely chronological. The objects are presented singly or grouped according to themes or materials. In the East Asian department

in particular, the paintings are shown in separate paintings galleries. Like the prints, lacquer objects and textiles, they are rotated every three to six months for reasons of conservation. Although the Museum für Asiatische Kunst consists primarily of objects prior to 1960, contemporary works of art are always shown as well, usually together with objects from the collections of ancient art.

How does this island of art fit with the concept of the Humboldt-Forum as an institution that will accept the themes of all cultures and enter into a dialogue with them? How are Asian art and art history defined, isolated, or integrated into the great issues of culture and history? How do works of art relate to everyday objects? These overarching questions are taken up at the Humboldt-Forum and at the same time point beyond it to

Design for the visible storage for South, Southeast, and Central Asia, with the Cave of the Ring-Bearing Doves, Ralph Appelbaum Associates/ malsyteufel, 2013

Portrait of a princess, India,
Jaipur, mid-18th century

the society, to the city of Berlin. At the Humboldt-Forum, these issues will find a platform
for international exchange, discussion, exhibitions and events that will provide ever new
approaches to them and thus provoke inspiring ways of thinking.

The exhibition concept for the Humboldt-Forum

At the Humboldt-Forum we have an opportunity to design a completely new museum.
We find ourselves not only in a spectacular building in a new, central location but also in
a new world. India, Indonesia, Japan, China and Korea are important economic and political powers, who are very conscious of the value of their art and culture. Presenting them

page 102
Seated Buddha, China,
7th or 8th century

Design for the exhibition area for Central Asia with the Cave of the Sword Bearers in the Cupola Hall, Ralph Appelbaum Associates/ malsyteufel, 2013

appropriately must therefore be the focus of our deliberations. In the process, several positions must be considered and balanced: On the one hand, Asian art must be shown in ways analogous to those employed for the art of Western cultures. On the other hand, they have to be embedded into the canon of art from all continents. Moreover, issues of how the works were acquired and of the legacy of colonialism must be considered. Different groups of visitors, who now come increasingly from Asian countries, have to be addressed and fascinated just like visitors from Europe who have no direct access to the art of Asia.

The "how" of the presentation will be crucial to that process. It matters less whether we follow a tradition from the early era of Asian museums in the West by attempting to

exhibit Asian art in its original context based on criteria of the traditional understanding of art in the country concerned. Younger Asian museum-goers are no more familiar with this approach than average visitors from other parts of the world. The Humboldt-Forum wants to discover new paths and break through the familiar framework with exciting dramatisations. The modern and contemporary art of Asian will play a central role in that. One important challenge for a museum of Asian art in the West is presenting and conveying the latest developments in Asia, as artists find their way between the tradition of their own culture and the demands of a globalized art world. At the same time, contemporary art can simplify a younger audience's access to the artistic treasuries of Asia, since famous artists such as Xu Bing, Hiroshi Sugimoto, Maqbul Fida Husain and Atul Dodiya, to name just a few examples, often refer in their art to older works from the history and culture of their own country. When we exhibit famous artists such as Subodh Gupta, Lee Ufan and Ai Weiwei prominently at the Humboldt-Forum, it demonstrates to visitors, especially those from Asia, that their art and artists are taken seriously here and contribute to the exhibitions.

In Berlin we can and must overcome the familiar and break free of the conventional framework. Precisely because the large museums of Asian countries take their lead from the famous museums of the West, with the result that a uniform style of presentation and design has emerged worldwide, we have to create something new in order to expand the scope and create possibilities for new ideas. Naturally, the tried and tested will have its place at the Humboldt-Forum along with the new, the different, and the contrary. Although in the future visitors will be coming in increasing numbers from Asia, the major-

Screen for the imperial throne,
China, ca. 1670–1700

ity of them will continue to be from Germany and Europe. They know hardly anything about Asian art. The museum was created more than a hundred years ago and has been continuously expanded in order to offer Western audiences an opportunity to become familiar with Asian art, to learn the main lines of Asian art history, and to understand the criteria of quality, the subject matter, and the contexts of this art, which are not easily recognisable. This original concern has lost none of its topicality today, particularly in a globalised world.

The planning and design of the new Museum für Asiatische Kunst have not yet been settled in all their details, but they have already come a long way. The few examples here are intended to indicate the outlines. It is very clear that the design will be more varied and the exhibition spaces less uniform than they are in Dahlem now. That is a conscious decision, influenced in part by the fact that the works of art will be presented far more often across genres within the large cultural regions. At the same time, the density of presentations will vary considerably.

Small goblet with openwork wall, China, late Ming dynasty, first quarter of the 17th century

The Museum für Asiatische Kunst offers a survey of the art of the large cultural regions of East, Central, South and Southeast Asia. There has always been intense exchange between and within these large regions, particularly when it comes to religion and art. To help orient the public, the exhibition is arranged according to geography as well as a loose and flexible chronology. Nevertheless, distributed over the exhibition area there are a number of connections to and interventions from the present, often in the form of temporary installations of contemporary art.

Given the unique quality and size of the Central Asian collection of the Museum für Asiatische Kunst, we will make particular use of its potential. It will serve as a hinge joining the museum's East and South Asian departments. The Central Asian collection was never intended or acquired as a pure art collection. A selection of just a few of its best works of art can therefore never do it justice. In the wake of four Prussian expeditions to Xinjiang (1902–14), hundreds of murals, sculptures, architectural pieces, and thousands of archaeological objects, paintings, and fragments of texts on paper and silk from the fifth to the fourteenth century came to Berlin. The collection thus represents an opportunity to tell the complete story of the religion, art, trade, intercultural exchange, linguistic diversity, and everyday life in the various cities along the Silk Road and the Buddhist caves of Xinjiang. In the central space beneath the large cupola designed by Friedrich August Stüler, known as the Cupola Room, which also serves as a connection between the South and East Asia departments, these central themes are presented succinctly. The full of material, which offers insights into vanished cultures that are equally fascinating for laypersons and scholars, will be seen in a dense landscape of spectacular vitrines and along the tall walls in a second room: the Southern Cube. The exhibition here will seem almost like a laboratory in which the visitor can study the progress of scholarship on Central Asia. The proposed design solutions are very promising.

Corresponding to this eight-metre-high hall, covering a floor area of 560 square metres, is the Northern Cube, in which the subject of art at the court of the Qianlong Emperor in eighteenth-century China is presented. Here the East Asian collections of the Ethnologisches Museum and the Museum für Asiatische Kunst will be closely intertwined

Suzuki Harunobu, Descending Geese of the Koto, 1765–66, sheet from the series Eight Views of Interiors

and their holdings displayed according to thematic perspectives. A large imperial throne with a screen, a masterpiece of the art of lacquerware, is the central exhibit. As supreme commander, the emperor documented his military victories in engravings. They were printed from copperplates prepared in Paris and Beijing based on models by European painters working at his court; thirty-four examples from the holdings of the Ethnologisches Museum are shown as an important document of Chinese-European relationships in the eighteenth century. The emperor was also a guardian of religion and moral: The enormous painting *The Buddha Preaching*, measuring 525 by 950 centimetres, which was commissioned from the court painter Ding Guanpeng (ca. 1706–70/71) for a temple on the palace grounds, testifies to this. Moreover, the emperor became an educated collector of art: He possessed the largest collection of art and curiosities that has ever existed anywhere in the world. Paintings and applied arts in the emperor's taste illustrate his passion for collecting.

In the adjacent Japanese section, a tearoom will occupy a central place, as was already the case in Dahlem; after all, the tea ceremony represents a crystallization point in the Japanese experience of the arts. Whereas Dahlem has had a traditional tearoom with tatami mats, paper-covered sliding doors, and shingle roof, at the Humboldt-Forum it will be a contemporary tearoom, in which everything will look different, though the traditionally prescribed proportions will be retained. Here too attention will be drawn to the subject of Zen and relationships between East and West. What does Zen mean in the Eastern world, and what form does it take when grappled with and appropriated in works by Western artists such as John Cage, Jack Kerouac or ZEN 49?

In the South and Southeast Asian areas, the exhibition at the Humboldt-Forum will also follow a new concept, which to some degree moves away from a purely art historical presentation. An entrance space will address the theme of the cult of fertility spirits and nature gods, which can be regarded as the substrate for all religion and art in South and Southeast Asia. Details of the design have not been definitively determined, but trees and ponds will certainly play a central role. In general, the exhibits will be contextualized far more, taking into account the fact that the majority of art from South Asia is religious art. For example, the sculptures are usually cultic images based on a ritual context. The arts and crafts of the Islamic era of the Indian subcontinent are particularly well suited to illustrating transcultural phenomena.

Both the Museum für Asiatische Kunst and the Ethnologisches Museum have collections of Southeast Asian art. Although a border will run between the two museums in this area, visitors will scarcely notice it on their tour. The prelude to the ethnological exhibition is also the connection to the Museum für Asiatische Kunst: dance and theatre, with shadow plays, masks, and marionettes from Indonesia, Thailand, Burma, India and China. It follows harmoniously on the fading out of the exhibition of Asian art with the plaster casts of the narrative reliefs from Angkor Wat in Cambodia. Whereas the purist exhibition in Dahlem did not feature casts, casts made from nineteenth-century papier mâché moulds will now present a state of these reliefs that in part differs considerably from that seen today. The fate of one of the most important monuments of humanity can be demonstrated graphically.

Every time a new museum is planned, the directors, curators, designers, and architects look for examples, ideas and inspiration in other museums. They want to know how others have done it and to see whether any of their ideas can be used. We too did this and will continue to do so. But it is a good sign that we neither can nor wish to fall back on something existing for the exhibition areas for the new Museum für Asiatische Kunst at the Humboldt-Forum. If we succeed in breaking new ground for the other presentations as well, we are on the way to opening for visitors a new window on a distant, foreign world and to making it possible for them to engage in a lively and active way with the art of Asia of the past and present, with its uniqueness, and with its current global interaction.

Bōki tearoom in the Ostasiatische Kunstsammlung, Museum für Asiatische Kunst, Berlin-Dahlem, 2012

Franco Stella, Berliner Schloss –
Humboldt-Forum, entrance hall,
section, 2013

Well Established. The Humboldt-Forum Staff Unit and the Humboldt Lab Dahlem: Planning and Implementation of Concepts and Projects

Bettina Probst/
Agnes Wegner

The Humboldt-Forum in the Berliner Schloss: two points of view?

The title of this publication already betrays the fact: We are concerned, to put it simply, with two things that have to come together: a forum and a palace. Both are currently under development. Two pillars support the entire project and the process: The Stiftung Berliner Schloss – Humboldtforum (Berlin Palace - Humboldtforum Foundation) stands for the building; the Stiftung Preußischer Kulturbesitz (Prussian Cultural Heritage Foundation), as the largest partner in this cooperation with the Zentral- und Landesbibliothek Berlin (Central and Regional Library Berlin) and the Humboldt-Universität zu Berlin, stands for the content.

The reconstruction of the Berliner Schloss should be recognisable not only as a historical reconstruction but also as something new: it will provide space for new content and for cultural encounters. On the one hand, it is about the palace as an architectural landmark that contributes to the identity of Berlin-Mitte; and on the other, it is about the opportunity to create in the Humboldt-Forum a site of world cultures with international influence. Both points of view open up a perspective on a common goal: the interplay of one's own historical identity and self-assurance in a globalised world. This unique opportunity will represent a great challenge for all of us.

Dialogue as a basic principle

The idea and objective of the Humboldt-Forum, with its function for dialogue and participation, has a direct effect on the path to its realisation that we intend to illuminate from different perspectives and follow together. Working with culture or different cultures also

page 113
Eight-headed dancing Hevajra, Cambodia, 12th or 13th century

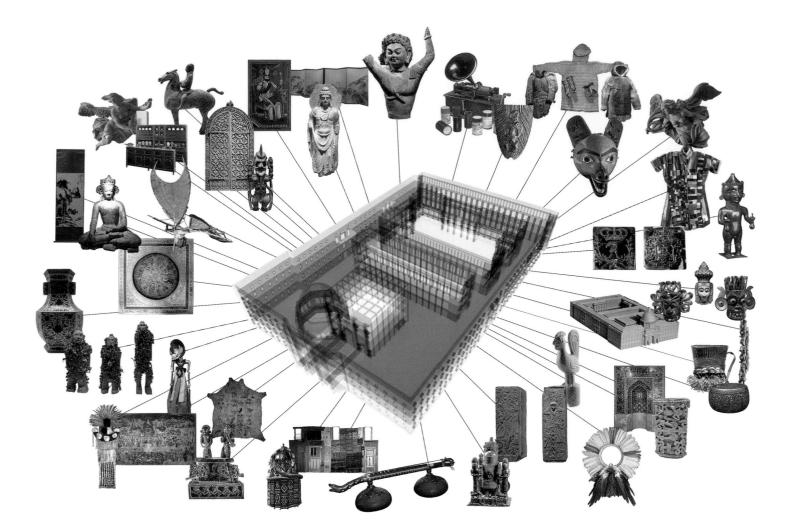

The collections of the Ethnologisches Museum and the Museum für Asiatische Kunst at the Humboldt-Forum, Master plan: Ralph Appelbaum Associates/malsyteufel, rendering, 2012

demands an organisational culture that enables the actors and partners to engage in a strong dialogue with one another. That means working closely together despite some differences in points of view, improving networking, and agreeing on coherent goals and a harmonised approach.

The essays in the present volume underscore very clearly that the Berliner Schloss and the Humboldt-Forum, and hence form and content, are not diametrically opposed. Nevertheless, the project as a whole is marked by manifold dualisms that seek to be connected: developer and user, history and present, nature and art, science and the public, Europe and non-European art and culture, museum and site for events. The list could be extended at will. What is certain is that this project is not only about the quality of the reconstruction, of the design of the museums and collections, of the events that take place in the forum, of scholarship, education, and science; it is also about the quality of the collaboration. That alone will produce results that will guide the Humboldt-Forum through the twenty-first century.

Hence we find ourselves in the middle of a highly exciting process that has to be controlled. As with many other large projects, there is not just one planner and decision maker but several of them, and they are responsible for different areas. Many people are contributing to the success of the project. More than thirty companies are already involved in the building or in the Stiftung Berliner Schloss – Humboldtforum and the Bundesamt für Bauwesen und Raumordnung (Federal Office Building and Regional Planning), including around 150 people involved in the planning process alone. By a rough estimate, at least three hundred people are actively involved in the reconstruction of the palace and the conception and planning of the Humboldt-Forum (in architecture, construction, design, communication, and creation either for the Stiftung Berliner Schloss – Humboldtforum or for the Stiftung Preußischer Kulturbesitz, with the Staatliche Museen zu Berlin (National Museums in Berlin), the Zentral- und Landesbibliothek Berlin, and Humboldt-Universität). If the activities of the Förderverein Berliner Schloss e. V. (Association Berliner Schloss) are included, there are even more!

Humboldt Lab Dahlem, Probebühne 1 (Rehearsal, Stage 1). Project: Museum der Gefässe (Museum of Vessels), March 2013

The Humboldt-Forum staff unit

With respect to construction, the users of the complex, and hence some of the people just mentioned, are coordinated by the Stiftung Berliner Schloss – Humboldtforum. For issues of content, which will be crucial for what will be exhibited and conveyed at the Humboldt-Forum, the Stiftung Preußischer Kulturbesitz set up the Humboldt-Forum headquarters, which will continue to develop and regulate the conception, planning and implementation of all the project participants. This work is done primarily within the foundation itself, together with the Ethnologisches Museum (Ethnological Museum) and the Museum für Asiatische Kunst (Asian Art Museum) of the Staatliche Museen zu Berlin and the corresponding departments and headquarters of the universities; it is also directed outward, however, in the diverse project-based relationships to our partners at the Humboldt-Forum and other third parties.

Beyond issues of content, it is dedicated to addressing structural, financial and organisational problems in order to ensure the development of the Humboldt-Forum in the coming years. Its primary task is thus to establish tasks and responsibilities, organizational structures and rules, procedures and standards, as well as schedules and budgets, all of which have to conform to or be harmonised with the schedules and other planning for the construction. No small part of that task is defining interfaces, for example, in architecture, design and media, and bringing together all the information necessary to organise the project, with the goal of making collaboration between all those involved as smooth and efficient as possible in the future.

To ensure quality in this process, various forms of competence, experience and expertise have to become involved. This role is played by a variety of committees and foundation boards, work and management groups, expert commissions and juries, management meetings and advisory boards. For example, the users have established a steering committee in order to reach agreement on forthcoming stages of developing plans for the content and design of all the facilities at the Humboldt-Forum. Various working groups also address issues of content or specific concepts for a variety of thematic issues, such as the art collection, the Archaeological Window, or the research, library, and service areas on the second floor.

Humboldt Lab Dahlem,
Probebühne 1 (Rehearsal
Stage 1), Project Musik sehen
"lichtklangphonogramm"
(Seeing Music "lightsound-
phonogram"), March 2013

One major focus is on working with designers: In November 2012, the master plan for the design of the museums at the Humboldt-Forum was presented by the design team of Ralph Appelbaum Associates/malsyteufel, thus reaching an important milestone. Nevertheless, it "merely" points the direction and does the preliminary work so that the "real" work of planning the design for the museums can proceed. It will be followed by the design of the libraries, including the Zentral- und Landesbibliothek, the two specialist libraries for the museum that are being combined at the Humboldt-Forum, and the Humboldt-Labor (Humboldt Laboratory) of the university once the corporate design for the building and for the areas on the second floor has been commissioned.

The headquarters stands for the long-term implementation of the content and design of the Humboldt-Forum, but also for cooperation with project participants and current and potential partners with an eye to the areas of education and outreach, media cooperation, and sponsoring. It is therefore an important interface within the project as a whole.

The Humboldt Lab Dahlem

Alongside the Humboldt-Forum Headquarters, the Humboldt Lab Dahlem operates as a kind of rehearsal stage. It was established in 2012 by the Stiftung Preußischer Kulturbesitz in collaboration with the Kulturstiftung des Bundes (Federal Cultural Foundation). A concentrated series of exhibition projects with a variety of themes and formats will be presented through 2015 at the Ethnologisches Museum and the Museum für Asiatische Kunst in Dahlem. This rapid sequence of experimental exhibitions will lead to a very concrete form of visibility: in a very literal sense, they are trying out and evaluating. Not just theoretically and on paper but in a very real way, radically practical experiences are being accumulated in a free, playful approach and then shared with both the profession and the public. The Humboldt Lab Dahlem is directed by Viola König, Martin Heller, Klaas Ruitenbeek and the office management staff; the team is being advised by a consulting group with members from a number of countries.

By means of the experimental impetus derived from working on the projects, the lab supplements and enriches the planning of the Ethnologisches Museum and the Museum für Asiatische Kunst for their presentation concept at the Humboldt-Forum. The exhibitions, presentations, interventions and installations are developed based on specific museum practices but also on themes that result from working on the master plan. They always set out from specific questions: How can a museum today, when faced with global changes, convey an approach to non-European art and culture that is as clear as it is well-grounded? Which substantial challenges does a contemporary presentation of collections between ethnology and art have to address?

The project methodology can vary. It permits close collaboration between both internal and external museum curators with designers, artists, and scholars. The initial results were tested on Probebühne 1 (Rehearsal Stage 1) from March to May 2013. For example, for the Museum der Gefässe (Museum of Vessels) project, the curator Nicola Lepp developed forms of presentations that cross cultures and collections and break them down according to chronology and region. At the same time, the medium of film was employed

in programmatic ways. In Bedeutungen schichten (Layering Meaning), Andreas Heller and an interdisciplinary team tried to enter and to illustrate the complex and multilayered world of meanings for selected exhibits. Musik sehen (Seeing Music) focused on the visual qualities that can be conveyed by an exhibition based on musical instruments from the ethnological collections and sound documents from the Phonogramm-Archiv (Phonogram Archive). Future projects will always take into account current developments internationally in scholarship, contemporary art and museum practices. At the same time, partners for collaboration and specific projects will be sought, particularly with an eye to the institutional transfer of the project results, not just for the Humboldt-Forum itself but also for comparable collections and museums.

For the Humboldt-Forum and its participants, the working methods of the lab and the headquarters contribute crucially to self-confidence regarding their own activities in the planning process by means of experiments and clarity, evaluation and critical question, the introduction of different viewpoints, and last but not least collaboration among many creative people and the participants in the projects.

Humboldt Lab Dahlem, Probe-bühne 1 (Rehearsal Stage 1), Project Springer "Spiegelkugel" (Knights "Mirror ball"), March 2013